ℱamily ℱavorites . . .

From across the Country

CONTENTS

Celebrity Favorites 2
Appetizers 11
Soups and Sandwiches 17
Breads and Rolls 23
Salads 33
Vegetables 44
Meats 53
Poultry 65
Fish and Seafood 75
Casseroles and Egg Dishes 86
Desserts, Pies and Cakes 97
Bars, Cookies and Candy 113
Pot Pourri 123
Helpful Hints 128

Editor
Shirley A. Burns

Celebrity Favorites

LARRY HAGMAN'S HOT AND SPICY SPAGHETTI
Makes about 1 ½ -2 quarts

- ¼ cup olive oil
- 2 medium size onions, peeled and chopped
- 3 cloves garlic, pressed
- 2 lbs. boneless beef neck meat, fat trimmed, cut in small cubes
- ½ tsp. cayenne pepper
- ¼ cup flour
- 1 bay leak
- 2 cans (8 ozs.) tomato sauce
- 2 cans (6 ozs.) tomato paste
- ½ lb. mushrooms, sliced
- 1 ½ cups water or beef stock (canned)
- 1 large lemon, squeezed
- 1 tsp. oregano
- 2 tsps. basil
- good handful parsley
- 1 ½ tsps. salt
- 1 T. Hungarian pepper (more or less to taste)

Heat olive oil in large skillet or stock pot. Saute onions and garlic until transparent. Lift out and reserve. Shake meat in paper bag with cayenne pepper, flour, salt and pepper. Brown meat on all sides in garlic flavored oil. Stir in remaining ingredients, blending well. Cook, uncovered, simmering for 3 hours and stirring occasionally. Toward end of cooking, add onions and garlic. Taste to correct seasonings. Serve over hot cooked spaghetti according to package instructions. Wonderful with French bread, green salad and your favorite red wine.

NOTE: If Hungarian pepper is not available, use red pepper flakes or chili pepper to give desired degree of ''hotness'' to sauce.

BOB BARKER'S MEXICAN CHILE CON QUESO

¾ cup chopped onion
⅓ cup chopped green pepper
1 lb. Velveeta cheese
4 oz. can pimentos with liquid

1 T. chili powder
1 tsp. garlic salt
butter

Saute onion and green pepper in butter. Melt Velveeta cheese and mix with onion and green pepper. Add can of pimentos with liquid. Season with chile powder and garlic salt.

Serve with Tortilla chips.

BETTY WHITE'S CHICKEN WINGS BAKE
Serves 6-8

4 lbs. chicken wings,
   cleaned
1 cup soy sauce

1 stick butter, melted
1 scant cup brown sugar
1 tsp. dry mustard

Arrange chicken in deep bowl. Prepare marinade by combining the rest of the ingredients. Pour marinade over chicken wings in bowl. Cover and leave at room temperature several hours. Turn chicken in marinade several times. Line shallow baking dish with aluminum foil. Arrange chicken wings in dish. Spoon enough sauce over wings to dampen them well. Bake, uncovered, in 375° F. oven about 1 hour, or until chicken is tender. Great as an appetizer or entrēe!

JERRY ORBACH'S PASTA AND BROCCOLI

2 T. olive oil
1 medium garlic clove, minced
1 ripe tomato, chopped
1 head broccoli, chopped

1 can chicken or beef broth
   (14 oz.)
1 lb. Rotelli macaroni
   salt, pepper and basil

In large skillet, saute garlic in oil; do not brown. Add tomato. Season with salt, pepper and basil to taste. Simmer over low heat about 10 minutes. Add chopped broccoli and broth. Cover and bring to a boil. Then simmer until broccoli is cooked; about 30 minutes or less. Cook macaroni according to directions; drain and add to broccoli.

4

SHIRLEY MACLAINE'S GOURMET LAMB STEW

Serves 6-8

5-6 lbs. boneless leg of lamb cut into 1½-inch cubes
1 T. lard
2 T. flour
1 clove garlic, minced
about 3 cups water
2 T. tomato paste
¼ tsp. lamb herbs or oregano
1½ tsps. salt
⅛ tsp. freshly ground black pepper
10 cubes sugar
1 T. hot water
3 T. sweet butter
1 small yellow onion, peeled and chopped
6 pearl onions, peeled and diced
2 small carrots, peeled and chopped
2 small turnips, peeled and chopped
1 tsp. sugar
1 T. parsley, chopped

Brown lamb in lard. Sprinkle flour over meat and cook a few minutes, stirring constantly. Add garlic; cook over very low heat until garlic begins to smell. Add water (enough to barely cover meat), tomato paste, lamb herbs, salt and pepper. Cover and simmer about 15 minutes. Meanwhile, put sugar lumps and 1 T. water in a small saucepan; heat over low heat until sugar carmelizes. Add sugar mixture to meat, stirring to blend well. Cover and simmer 30 minutes, stirring occasionally. Melt butter over low heat; add vegetables; sprinkle with sugar. Add vegetables to lamb; cover and cook, simmering about 30 minutes, or until vegetables and lamb are tender. Remove vegetables and lamb to a platter. Skim off surface fat before pouring sauce over meat. Garnish with parsley. Serve with crusty French bread and tossed green salad.

GINNIE NEWHART'S CARROT MOLD

1½ cups carrot, grated
1 cup brown sugar
½ cup soft margarine
½ tsp. baking powder
½ tsp. salt
1 egg beaten
1 cup all-purpose flour

Combine all ingredients; mix well. Place in greased 5½-cup ring mold. Bake in preheated 350° F. oven about 45 minutes. Unmold. Serve on platter with cooked green peas in the center.

NOTE: Ginnie comments, ''I usually make 3 or 4 of these, one to use and others to freeze. My family loves it. The ring looks so pretty with a green vegetable. Great with poultry, beef or fish.''

5

LIZA MINNELLI'S POTATO SHELLS

4 small, long, slender baking
potatoes
about 4 tsp. sweet butter
salt to taste
1 cup dairy sour cream (more if
needed)

4 T. caviar
1 jigger vodka
freshly ground pepper to
taste

Scrub and dry potatoes. Rub skins lightly with fat. Bake in preheated 425 degree oven about 1 ¼ hours, or until inside is soft and skin is crunchy. Cut potatoes in half lengthwise. Remove about half of the potato, put ½ tsp. butter in each shell and a light sprinkling of salt and freshly ground pepper. Fill each shell with sour cream. Top with 1 T. caviar and sprinkle with vodka. Serve at once as finger food to go with cocktails. Serves 8.

NOTE: Potato shells can be made as a dinner accompaniment by removing all the potato, flavoring it with butter, salt and pepper, then restuffing and double baking it before adding sour cream, caviar and vodka.

MOO GOO GAI PAN, HOUSE OF PERRY COMO
Serves 4

½ lb. fresh mushrooms
1 partially frozen chicken
breast, skinned, split and
boned
1 egg white, lightly beaten
1 tsp. salt
⅛ tsp. ground white pepper
4 T. vegetable oil
½ tsp. sugar (optional)
2½ cups celery, thinly sliced

1 can (8½ oz.) water
chestnuts, drained and thinly
sliced
1 pkg. (6 oz.) frozen snow
peas
or ½ lb. fresh snow peas
½ cup scallions, sliced
½ tsp. garlic, finely minced
2 tsps. soy sauce

Rinse, pat dry and slice fresh mushrooms; set aside. With Chinese meat cleaver or sharp knife, thinly slice chicken into ¼ inch strips. In a small bowl, combine egg white, cornstarch, sherry, ½ tsp. of salt and white pepper; blend well. In a wok or large skillet, heat 2 T. of vegetable oil. Add mushrooms, celery, water chestnuts, snow peas and remaining salt; sauté 5 minutes. Remove vegetables from wok; reserve. Heat remaining 2 T. vegetable oil in wok. Add scallions, garlic and chicken; cook over high heat, stir-frying constantly. Stir in soy sauce, sugar and vegetable mixture; cook 2 minutes longer, stirring often. Remove to a heated platter. Serve at once over hot cooked rice.

DOM DELUISE'S BLUEBERRY CHEESECAKE
Serves 10-12

1 baked 10-inch pie crust or
prepare as follows:
1 small jar Macadamia nuts
crushed in blender or with
rolling pin between
waxed paper

1 cup flour
¼ cup brown sugar, firmly
packed
¼ lb. sweet butter, softened

Combine all ingredients; mix well. Press into a 10-inch spring form pan. Bake in preheated 400° F. oven 10-15 minutes.

FOR THE FILLING
3 pkgs. (8 ozs.) cream cheese
1 cup sugar

4 eggs, room temperature
1 tsp. pure vanilla extract

Crumble cheese in large mixing bowl. Add remaining ingredients. Beat at high speed with portable mixer until well blended and smooth, about 5 minutes. Pour over crust. Bake at 350° F. 40 minutes, or until set. Cool 10 minutes.

GENE KELLY'S REAL IRISH STEW
Serves 6-8

3 lbs. lean boneless lamb
(shoulder or leg), cut in
1½-inch cubes
1 T. vegetable oil
about 3 cups water
2 onions
2 tsps. salt
¼ tsp. freshly ground pepper

bay leaf
2 turnips, peeled and cut in
large pieces
6 carrots, peeled and cut in
chunks
3 cups Irish potatoes, diced
2 T. fresh parsley, minced

Sprinkle lamb cubes with salt and pepper. Brown meat on all sides in oil in large skillet. Remove skillet from heat; add water to cover meat. Add onion, salt, pepper and bay leaf; cover and simmer until meat is tender about 1½ hours. Add remaining vegetables; cover and cook until vegetables are tender, about 35 minutes. Remove cover during last 15 minutes of cooking time to reduce the stock. Taste to correct seasonings. Spoon lamb and vegetables into deep serving dish. Spoon juice over lamb and vegetables. For a touch of the "green," garnish with parsley. Serve piping hot, alone, or with prepared horseradish and slabs of dark or crusty white bread and butter.

SOPHIA LOREN'S PIZZA ALLA NAPOLETANA

Dough;
2 cups flour
1 tsp. salt
1 tsp. olive oil
1 pkg. active dry yeast,
       dissolved in 1 ¼ cups lukewarm water

Garniture:
tomato sauce or canned marinara sauce, or peeled,
   chopped tomatoes, mushrooms, small tin
   filleted anchovies or sliced sweet Italian sausage,
   salmi or thin strips prosciutto ham
dried sweet basil
freshly grated Parmesan cheese
freshly ground pepper to taste
2-3 T. olive oil
mozzarella cheese

Place flour and salt on board. Add dissolved yeast. Knead
thoroughly, add oil, continue kneading until smooth. Place in
lightly greased bowl and cover. Set in warm place about 3
hours, or until dough doubles in bulk. Flatten, roll out dough
into a 10-inch disc about ½ -inch thick. Spread surface with
your choice of garniture. Heat olive oil in large, cast-iron
skillet. When oil is sizzling, add pizza. Cook over medium
flame about 10 minutes, or until golden and topping is
bubbly. Serve immediately. Serves 4.

FRED ASTAIRE'S CHICKEN SOUP WITH HOMEMADE NOODLES
Serves 6-8

FOR THE NOODLES

½ tsp. salt

2 eggs, slightly beaten

2 scant cups unsifted all-purpose flour

Add salt to eggs; add eggs to flour. Mix thoroughly with wooden spoon until dough leaves the sides of the bowl. (Dough should be fairly stiff.) Turn out on lightly floured board; knead lightly until smooth and elastic. Roll out dough with floured rolling pin to ⅛ thickness. Let dough stand until noodle sheet feels dry, about 30 minutes. Use a sharp knife to cut dough into narrow strips. Cut a few at a time, tossing lightly to separate strands. Allow to dry completely, about 1 hour, before storing in covered glass jar or plastic bag. When ready to use, drop in rapidly boiling salted water or soup. Cook about 10 minutes.

FOR THE SOUP

1 plump dressed chicken weighing 4 to 5 lbs.

2 cleaned chicken feet (optional)

about 4 quarts water

8 peppercorns, bruised

2 cloves

1 small onion, peeled and chopped

1 T. salt

6-8 sprigs parsley

2 stalks celery

2 bay leaves

2 eggs (with shells)

1 T. ice water

Wash chicken; cut into serving pieces. Scald and skin chicken feet. Put Chicken and feet in cold water; bring to a boil. Skim thoroughly. Simmer until chicken is tender, about 1½ hours. Add remaining ingredients except eggs and ice water. Cook 15 minutes. Strain and cool. Remove and discard chicken feet, reserve chicken. Refrigerate until ready to use. Remove layer of congealed chicken fat that forms on the top; reserve fat for cooking or flavoring liver pâté. Reheat broth and clarify by adding 2 beaten eggs and broken eggshells to the stock. Place over low heat and stir constantly until the broth is simmering. Boil 2 minutes. Add 1 T. ice water; set aside for 10 minutes. Then strain through a double thickness of cheesecloth placed over a fine strainer. Reheat broth, adding noodles; simmer until noodles are cooked. Taste soup to correct seasonings.

Appetizers

PARTY CHEESE BALL

2 8-oz. pkg. cream cheese
  softened
2 cups shredded sharp cheddar
  cheese
1 T. chopped pimiento
1 T. chopped green pepper
1 T. minced onion

1 tsp. lemon juice
2 tsp. worcestershire sauce
  dash cayenne pepper
  dash of salt
  finely chopped pecans

Blend cheese thoroughly. Add the pimiento, green pepper, onion, Worcestershire sauce, lemon juice, cayenne pepper and salt. Mix well, then chill, shape into a ball and roll in pecans. Keep chilled until ready to serve. Serve with assorted crackers.

Mrs. Howard Lundeen   Sun City, Arizona

CRAB MEAT SPREAD

1 can (7 oz.) crab meat
1 pkg. (8 oz.) cream cheese

½ cup barbeque sauce with
  horseradish, to taste

Spread softened cream cheese on serving tray, sprinkle with well drained crab meat and pour barbeque sauce over top. Serve with seasoned crackers to spread it on.

Mrs. Carol Livingston   Ballwin, Missouri

POTATO CHIP DIP

1 lb. ground beef
1 lb. Velveeta cheese

1 can Old El Paso tomatoes and
  green chilies

Brown ground beef; drain fat. Melt cheese, small bits at a time, with the meat on the stove. After all of the cheese has been melted, add the tomatoes and green chilies. Keep on low heat until the mixture is heated through. Pour into chip and dip bowl. Tastes best when served warm. Serve with chips or crackers. (This dip is a bit "runny" at first, but tends to thicken up after it cools down a little.)

Deane Lee   Carmel, Indiana

MUSHROOM CROUSTADES

24 thin slices French bread · · · · · · · · · · 2 tps. melted butter

Using cookie cutter, cut 3 inch rounds of bread, trimming crust if necessary. Coat inside of tiny muffin tins with melted butter and mold bread rounds into each cup. Bake at 400 degrees about 10 minutes or until lightly golden. Remove and let cool. (Note—these freeze very well.)

Mushroom Filling:

3 T. finely chopped shallots	1 tsp. finely chopped parsley
½ lb. mushrooms finely chopped	1½ tsp. finely chopped chives
2 T. flour	½ tsp. lemon juice
1 cup whipping cream	Parmesan cheese
⅛ tsp. cayenne pepper	4 T. butter
½ tsp. salt	

In skillet, melt 4 T. butter, add shallots. Stir constantly over heat 4 minutes; do not brown. Add mushrooms and coat thoroughly with butter, cooking until all moisture evaporates, 10-15 minutes. Remove from heat, add flour and stir. Immediately pour cream over, stirring constantly. Bring mixture to a boil; turn down heat and cook 1 minute. Remove from heat and stir in remaining ingredients. Transfer to covered bowl; refrigerate until ready to use. Fill croustades with mushroom mixture. Sprinkle with Parmesan cheese; dot with butter. Place on cookie sheet. Bake at 350 degrees for 10 minutes. Put under broiler for the last minute. Makes 24.

Barbara Kraetsch

Wauwatosa, Wisconsin

SHRIMP DIP

½ cup mayonnaise	1 can miniature shrimp or
½ cup diced celery	frozen shrimp
2 T. minced dry onions or ¼ cup	1½ T. lemon juice
fresh diced onions	1 pkg. (8 oz.) cream cheese, softened

Cream together cream cheese and mayonnaise. Mix lemon juice with shrimp and let sit for a few minutes. Add celery and onion to cream cheese mixture. Fold in shrimp. Refrigerate for 24 hours. Add a little milk before serving if too thick.

Julie Abraham

Kentwood, Michigan

MEXICAN DIP

3 medium ripe avocados
2 T. lemon juice
1 pkg. taco seasoning mix
½ tsp. salt
2 medium tomatoes, chopped
6 oz. can black olives, chopped
  tortilla chips

1 8 oz. pkg. cheddar cheese, shredded
2 cans plain or jalapeno bean dip
4 green onions, chopped
¼ tsp. pepper
1 cup sour cream
½ cup Miracle Whip

Mash avocado with lemon juice, salt and pepper; combine sour cream, Miracle Whip and taco seasoning mix. Spread bean dip on platter, top with avocado mix; top with sour cream mix. Sprinkle top with layers of onion, tomatoes, olives and cheese; chill, serve with tortilla chips.

Linda Vanover   Manchester, Missouri

TERIYAKI STEAK APPETIZERS

1 ½ lb. sirloin steak
½ cup salad oil
¼ cup liquid honey

½ cup finely chopped Spanish onion
1 clove of garlic, crushed
½ tsp. ginger

Cut steak into long ¹⁄₁₆ inch strips across the grain. Combine remaining ingredients in large flat pan; add steak strips. Marinate strips for several hours. Lift strips out of marinade; shake to remove excess. Thread strips on metal skewers. Place on grill; broil over medium heat just until well browned, turning and brushing with marinade. Serve hot.

Betty DeHaven   Mobile, Alabama

PARTY ONION ROUNDS

Small white bread rounds
Mayonnaise

Thinly sliced sweet onion
Grated Parmesan cheese

Spread bread with mayonnaise; top with onion slice. Spread again with mayonnaise, sprinkle with cheese. Place on cookie sheets, Broil till brown. Watch carefully. May be prepared ahead of time; refrigerate until ready to broil.

Dorothy Rees   Tucson, Arizona

BACON WRAP-AROUNDS

10 strips bacon, cut in half
20 raw scallops

Partially cook bacon. Wrap each bacon slice around a raw scallop and broil until bacon is crisp. Serve with toothpicks.
Makes 20 appetizers

Fran Tucker   Washington, D.C.

 **Family Favorite**

Appetizer
Notes

Ask the person whose card appears on the inside front cover of this book for a recipe form to submit your family favorite appetizer for next year's national cookbook.

Soups and Sandwiches

CHEESE SOUP

½ cup carrot, finely chopped
½ cup onion, finely chopped
¼ cup celery, finely chopped
2 T. butter
¼ cup all purpose flour

1 cup chicken broth
¼ tsp. salt
2 cups light cream or milk
1½ cups (6 oz.) American
   cheese, shredded

In covered sauce pan cook carrot, onion, celery in butter over low heat till tender. Stir in flour. Add broth and salt. Cook and stir till thickened and bubbly. Stir in cream or milk and cheese till cheese melts and soup is heated through. DO NOT BOIL. Makes 4 to 6 servings.

Alice Anderson

Waunakee, Wisconsin

CLAM CHOWDER

1 medium potato, peeled and
   diced
½ cup water
1 8 oz. can minced clams
   (reserve liquid)

1 medium onion, chopped
3 T. butter
1 pt. half and half cream
Salt and pepper to taste
2 tsp. chopped parsley

Place potato in saucepan with water, add liquid from clams. Cook for 4 min. and add onion. Cook another 2 minutes. Add clams, butter, cream, salt, pepper and parsley. Do not overboil but simmer for 30 minutes.

Rose Meyer

St. Louis, Missouri

SENEGALESE SOUP

2 cans cream of chicken soup
3 cups milk

½ tsp. curry powder
2 T. toasted coconut

Combine soup, milk and curry powder in medium saucepan; cook over medium heat just until bubbly. Beat with rotary beater until creamy and smooth. Pour into 8 small bowls or cups. Sprinkle with coconut. Serves 8.

Ruby Potts

Reno, Nevada

CREAM OF ASPARAGUS SOUP

¾ lb. fresh asparagus, cut into 1-inch pieces and
    steamed until tender
1 medium onion, quartered
5 T. butter
1 tsp. salt
½ tsp. white pepper
6 cups beef bouillon
2 cups light cream

Top with fresh onion greens or ground nutmeg. Puree asparagus and mince onion set aside. Melt butter in a 4-quart stockpot. Add onion and sauté for 2 minutes, stirring occasionally. Add asparagus, salt, and pepper; mix well. Stir in beef bouillon. Simmer for 20 minutes. Stir in cream. Simmer just to heat through. Pour into 6 soup bowls. Top with onion or ground nutmeg.

Mary Wilson   Cedar Rapids, Iowa

EGG DROP SOUP

Prepare chicken broth as follows:

4 to 5 lb. stewing chicken	2 sticks celery
2 qt. hot water	1 medium onion
2 tsp. salt	1 carrot

Bring to a boil, remove foam, cover. Simmer for 2 to 3 hours. Beat 4 eggs. Mix together with:

2 T. bread crumbs	2 T. Parmesan cheese

Add to boiling broth, stirring continuously until eggs are set. Remove from heat.

Mary Ross   Dallas, Texas

FRESH PEA SOUP WITH CROUTONS

3 T. unsalted butter	6 leaves fresh tarragon, finely chopped
2 cups fresh or frozen peas	
1 medium-size head butter lettuce, chopped	Croutons (½-inch cubes of French bread sautéed in olive oil until brown and crisp)
4 scallions, chopped	
6 cups chicken stock or water salt and pepper to taste	Health cream or crème fraiche (optional)

Melt butter in pot and add peas, lettuce and scallions. Cook over medium low heat for 5 minutes. Do not brown them. Add stock, bring to boil, reduce to simmer and cook until peas are tender, 10 to 15 minutes. Puree soup in blender or food processor. Season with salt and pepper and add tarragon. Serve hot or cold with croutons. You can enrich soup with a few tablespoons of heavy cream, if you wish.

Jerlyn Lawson   Augusta, Georgia

MOM'S BEEF SANDWICH

2 lbs. ground beef	2 T. mustard
1 can cornbeef	1-2 T. brown sugar
½ cup ketchup	Salt and pepper to taste

Brown ground beef and drain. Add cornbeef, ketchup, mustard, brown sugar, salt and pepper. Mix well into cooked ground beef and heat well. Serve on buns.

Kathryn Burns   Clinton, Maryland

CHEESE SOUP

4 bouillon cubes (beef or chicken)	1 pkg. (20 oz.) frozen Italian blend vegetables
1 qt. water	2 cans Cream of Chicken soup
2½ cups cubed potatoes	1 lb. Velveeta cheese, cut into chunks
1 cup celery, diced	
1 cup onion, diced	

Combine bouillon cubes, water, potatoes, celery and onion and cook covered about 20 minutes or till tender. Add package of vegetables. Cook about 10 minutes. Add soup and cheese. Stir. Soup is ready to serve when cheese is melted. Makes about 4 quarts.

Grace Ann Withers   Louisville, Kentucky

BEST SLOPPY JOES IN THE MIDWEST

3½ lbs. ground beef	½ cup vinegar
½ green pepper, chopped	2 T. salt
1 medium onion, chopped	½ cup sugar
1 cup celery, chopped	¼ cup prepared mustard
3 small cans tomato paste	⅓ tsp. cloves
3 tomato paste cans of water	½ cup bread crumbs
1 T. Worcestershire	

Brown meat and drain. In same skillet cook vegetables until tender. Add meat and all other ingredients and mix well. Simmer 30 minutes, stirring occasionally.

Barbara Kraetsch   Wauwatosa, Wisconsin

VEGETABLE SOUP

1 17 oz. can whole kernel corn with liquid	1 46 oz. can tomato juice
1 cup diced carrot	2 T. butter
1 cup celery, diced	3 cups water
2 T. minced onion	2 tsp. sugar
2 potatoes, sliced	Salt and pepper to taste
	1 10 oz. package frozen peas

In a stockpot, combine all ingredients except peas. Bring to a boil. Reduce heat and simmer, uncovered, 45 minutes. Add peas and simmer an additional 3-5 minutes.

Mrs. Cavett Woods   Carmel, Indiana

21

*F*amily *F*avorite Soup and Sandwich Notes

Ask the person whose card appears on the inside front cover of this book for a recipe form to submit your family favorite soups and sandwiches for next year's national cookbook.

Breads and Rolls

CARAWAY RYE BREAD

3 cups sifted all purpose flour
2 pkg. dry yeast
1 T. caraway seeds
2 cups water

½ cup brown sugar
1 T. shortening
1 tsp. salt
2½ cups rye flour

In large mixing bowl combine 2¼ cups flour, yeast, and caraway seeds. Heat water, brown sugar, shortening and salt until warm, stirring to melt shortening. Add to dry ingredients and on low speed beat about 30 seconds. Scrape sides of bowl constantly. Beat another 3 minutes on high speed. Measure rye flour and stir to mix. Hand stir. Add enough of the remaining all purpose flour to make moderately stiff dough. Turn on lightly floured surface and knead until smooth. In greased bowl turn dough to grease all surfaces. Cover and let rise until bulk doubles, about 1½ hours. Punch down dough and divide in half. Cover and allow to rest about 10 minutes. Shape into 2 round loaves and place on large greased baking sheet. Cover and allow to rise until bulk doubles, about 40 minutes. Bake 40 to 45 minutes in 350 degree oven.

Bettie Maxwell

Billings, Montana

MONKEY BREAD

4 tubes buttermilk biscuits, 10 count each
1⅓ cups sugar, divided

1 stick margarine
a tsp. vanilla
2 tsps. cinnamon, divided

Cut each biscuit into 4 pieces. Mix together ⅔ cup sugar and 1 tsp. cinnamon. Put cinnamon mixture in a brown paper bag or container with tight-fitting lid. Drop 4 to 6 pieces of dough into the bag or container. Shake until each piece is coated with sugar-cinnamon mixture. Remove from bag; drop into a buttered tube pan. Repeat process until all pieces of dough have been used. In a small saucepan, melt margarine. Add remaining ⅔ cup sugar, remaining 1 tsp. cinnamon and vanilla. Bring to boil. Pour syrup over biscuit pieces in prepared pan. Bake in 350° for 40 minutes. Remove from oven; immediately invert baking dish on serving platter. Serve in place of coffeecake and sweet rolls.

Mrs. Edward Schwab

Carmel, Indiana

WHITE BREAD

½ cup margarine
2 cups milk, heated
¼ cup sugar
2 tsp. salt
1 egg
1 pkg. dry yeast
5½ cups flour

Heat margarine; add milk, sugar and salt. Beat egg in large bowl; add hot mixture. When milk mixture is comfortable to wrist (warmer than room temperature), add yeast and dissolve. Add half the flour and mix with wooden spoon. Add rest of flour and blend. Divide dough and place in 2 greased bowls. Grease tops of dough, cover and let rise in warm place for 2 hours. Knead vigorously, and place in 2 greased loaf pans to rise for ½ hour. Bake at 350° for 40-50 minutes.

Mrs. John Jenkins   Louisville, Mississippi

25

PINEAPPLE-CHEESE LOAF

2 cups sifted flour
¾ cup sugar
1 T. baking powder
½ tsp. salt
½ cup grated sharp cheddar
cheese

½ cup chopped walnuts
1 cup drained crushed
pineapple (drain well)
2 T. melted butter
1 egg beaten

Sift together flour, sugar, baking powder and salt. Add cheese and nuts and toss together. Stir the pineapple and butter into the beaten egg; add to dry ingredients. Blend well by hand (do not use mixer) and pour into greased bread pan. Bake 1 hour at 350 degrees. Turn out on wire rack to cool. When cool wrap well and store until the next day. Flavor is better the second day.

Barbara Kraetsch   Wauwatosa, Wisconsin

WOODEN SPOON COFFEE CAKE

1 loaf frozen white bread
½ cup soft butter (no substitute)
¼ cup brown sugar firmly packed
¼ cup white sugar

¼ cup flour
½ tsp. vanilla
1 tsp. cinnamon
¼ cup nuts

Thaw and soften dough. Shape into round ball and flatten slightly. Place in greased 9 inch round layer pan. Let rise in warm place until doubled. Before baking, with end of wooden spoon or thumb or index finger, punch holes in dough. Combine butter, sugars, flour and vanilla. Fill each hole with this mixture. Continue to punch holes in dough and fill until all the mixture is used. Sprinkle top with cinnamon and nuts. Bake immediately at 350 degrees about 30 minutes or until golden brown and loaf sounds hollow when tapped. Immediately remove from pan. Serve warm.

Jan Nelson   Burnsville, Minnesota

BEER BREAD

1 can dark beer
2 T. sugar

3 cups self-rising flour

Blend sugar into beer. Stir in flour one cup at a time. Grease loaf pan. Pour in batter. Bake at 350 degrees for 1 hour. Turn out after cooling in pan for 10 minutes. Makes one loaf.

Nancy Bryant   Lexington, Kentucky

MERRY CHERRY SWEET BREAD

2½ cups sifted flour
2 tsp. baking powder
½ tsp. baking soda
1 tsp. salt
½ cup golden raisins
½ cup chopped red and green
   candied cheeries

1 cup chopped walnuts
¾ cup butter or margarine
1½ cups sugar
2 eggs
1 cup orange juice

Sift together flour, baking powder, baking soda and salt. Sprinkle 1 cup of mixture over combined fruits and nuts. Cream butter and sugar thoroughly. Add eggs and beat until light and fluffy. Add dry ingredients and orange juice, stirring until just blended. Fold in floured nuts and fruit. Spoon batter into well greased 9 inch tube pan. Bake at 350° for 1 hour or until center tests done. Cool for 5 minutes and remove from pan. Frost and top with nuts if desired. Makes 12 to 14 servings.

Jane Hilleman   Bridgeton, Missouri

QUICK SALLY LUNN

2 eggs, separated
½ cup sugar
2 cups flour, sifted
3 tsp. baking powder

½ tsp. salt
¾ cup milk
2 T. butter, melted
¼ cup sugar

Beat egg yolks with sugar. Mix flour, baking powder and salt. Add dry ingredients to sugar mixture, alternately with milk. Add melted butter. Beat egg whites until stiff and fold into batter. Pour into greased loaf pan. Sprinkle sugar on top. Bake 40-45 minutes at 350°.

Gloria Seaburg   West Miffin, Pennsylvania

POPOVERS

1 cup flour
1 cup milk
3 T. salad oil

½ tsp. salt
3 eggs

Put all ingredients in blender and blend well. Place greased muffin tins in oven for 10 minutes. Pour batter into hot muffin tins, filling each ⅔ full. Bake for 15 min. at 400°, reduce heat to 350° and continue cooking 30 minutes. DO NOT OPEN oven door until cooking time is finished. Yields 8-10 popovers.

Evelyn Schroeder   Provo, Utah

CARROT BREAD

2 eggs	1 tsp. baking soda
¾ cup salad oil	1 tsp. cinnamon
1 cup sugar	¾ tsp. salt
1½ cups flour	½ cup nuts
1½ cups grated raw carrot	

Beat eggs, add sugar and beat until well blended. Add oil and beat well again. Combine dry ingredients and add to egg and sugar mixture. Fold in carrots and nuts. Bake at 325° for 45 minutes to 1 hour.

Ann Beullens   Kansas, Missouri

CINNAMON ROLLS

2½ cups warm water	margarine
2 pkgs. yeast	brown sugar
1 reg. size yellow cake mix	cinnamon
2 eggs	nuts
4½ cups flour (plus at least 1 cup more while kneading)	raisins (optional)

Dissolve yeast in warm water. Add cake mix, eggs and flour; mix well. Knead until smooth, about 5 minutes; add more flour as you knead so dough isn't sticky. Let rise in warm place until double. Roll to ¼ inch thickness and spread with soft margarine, sprinkle brown sugar, cinnamon, nuts and raisins. Roll up like jelly roll and cut in ½ inch slices. Spread more margarine and brown sugar evenly in two 9x13 inch pans. Place rolls on top and let rise until double in size. Bake at 350° for 20 to 30 minutes. Frost if desired. Makes at least 24 rolls.

Judy Sharp   Chesterfield, Missouri

CORN BREAD

1 T. oil	1 tsp. baking soda
2 eggs	2 cups white water-ground
2 cups buttermilk	cornmeal
	1 tsp. salt

Preheat oven to 450°. Generously grease 9 inch square pan with oil. Heat in hot oven while mixing batter. Beat eggs, buttermilk and soda. Add cornmeal; beat well. Add salt. Pour into hot pan, bake 20-25 minutes.

Marlene Robinson   Lancaster, Pennsylvania

28

COFFEE CAKE

2 cups brown sugar	1 tsp. baking soda
½ cup shortening or oil	1 tsp. baking powder
2 eggs	1 tsp. cinnamon
1 cup buttermilk	¼ tsp. cloves (optional)
2 cups sifted flour	1 cup chopped nuts

Cream sugar and oil slightly, add eggs and buttermilk. Stir in dry ingredients until well blended. Pour into a well greased and floured 9x9 inch pan. Bake for 50 minutes at 325°.

Linda Walker   Kansas City, Kansas

BISHOP'S BREAD

1 ½ cups sifted flour	1 cup dates, finely chopped
½ tsp. baking powder	1 cup candied cherries,
¼ tsp. salt	chopped
⅔ cup chocolate chips	3 eggs
2 cups walnuts, chopped	1 cup sugar

Line bottom of loaf pan with waxed paper. Grease paper and sides of pan. Sift flour, baking powder and salt together. Stir in chocolate chips, walnuts, dates and cherries until well coated with flour. In large bowl, beat eggs well; gradually beat in all sugar. Fold in flour mixture and pour into loaf pan. Bake 1 ½ hours or until well done at 325°. Cool in pan. Remove when cool and wrap in foil to store.

Jackie Davis   Columbia, South Carolina

CRANBERRY BREAD

2 cups flour	½ cup nuts, chopped
¾ cup sugar	1 cup fresh or frozen cranber-
1 ½ tsp. baking powder	ries, chopped
1 tsp. salt	1 egg, beaten
½ tsp. soda	¾ cup orange juice
	2 T. salad oil

Preheat oven to 350°. Sift dry ingredients together. Stir in nuts and cranberries. Add remaining ingredients and blend until thoroughly moistened. Bake in greased, floured loaf pan 50 minutes or until golden brown.

Sylvia Sanders   Sioux Falls, South Dakota

PECAN ROLLS

     1 cup whole pecans
     ½ cup milk
     4 T. butter
     ⅓ cup granulated sugar
     ½ tsp. salt
     1 large egg at room temperature, lightly beaten
     ½ cup warm water (105 to 115°)
     1 package active dry yeast
     1 tsp. granulated sugar
  2 ½ to 3 cups unbleached all-purpose flour
     3 T. melted butter
     1 tsp. ground cinnamon
     6 T. granulated sugar
     ½ cup packed dark brown sugar

Chop pecans and set aside. Pour milk into a saucepan; and scald. Add the 4 T. butter, ⅓ cup sugar, and ½ tsp. salt; stir until butter melts. Cool to room temp. Stir in egg; set aside. Pour water into a measuring cup. Sprinkle yeast and 1 tsp. sugar over water; stir to dissolve yeast. Place in a draft-free area about 5 minutes. Add milk to yeast mixture and mix. Add 1 cup of flour at a time and mix well. Turn dough out onto a lightly floured board; gather into a ball. Place dough in a greased bowl; turn to grease top. Cover with a damp towel. Place in a draft-free area until double in bulk, about 1 ½ hours. Turn out onto a lightly floured surface. Roll out into an 8x16 inch rectangle. Brush the top with melted butter. Combine cinnamon and sugar. Sprinkle over dough. Roll up jelly-roll fashion from the long side. Cut into 12-cup pieces. Generously grease a 12-cup muffin pan. Sprinkle brown sugar in the bottom of each pan. Divide pecans among pans. Place a piece of dough, cut-side down, in each pan. Cover and let rise for 30 min. in a draft-free area. Preheat oven to 375°. Bake for 15 min. Invert rolls on a baking rack to cool.

Ida Benson   Alexandria, Virginia

 # Family Favorite   Breads and Rolls
Notes

Ask the person whose card appears on the inside front cover of this book for a recipe form to submit your family favorite bread and rolls for next year's national cookbook.

Salads

CORNED BEEF SALAD

1 pkg. Lemon jello   1 cup hot water

Mix together and let cool.

¾ cup mayonnaise
1 cup sour cream
3 hard boiled eggs, chopped
1 small onion, chopped or minced

1 small green pepper, chopped
1 can corned beef, crumbled
1 tsp. horseradish

Mix together and add to cooled jello. Place in a 9x13 inch pan and refrigerate.

Merle Healy   Lake Stevens, Washington

TUNA SALAD

1 head lettuce, shredded
1 cucumber, sliced
2 medium tomatoes, diced
1 can (medium) tuna, drained & flaked

½ pkg. (4 oz.) cooked elbow noodles, chilled
2 T. fresh parsley, chopped fine
½ cup 1,000 Island Dressing

Put all ingredients, except dressing, in bowl. Toss. Then mix in 1,000 Island Dressing. Use more or less depending on taste. Serve immediately.

Bill Smith   Victoria, Texas

CAULIFLOWER SALAD

1 head of cauliflower, chopped fine
6 strips bacon, fried crisp
¾ cup sugar
1 small onion, chopped

1 head lettuce, chopped fine
1 cup Kraft Miracle Whip
2 sticks celery, chopped

Layer cauliflower, lettuce, celery and onion; place bacon on top of layers. Mix Miracle Whip and sugar until well mixed. Pour over other ingredients. Let stand over night. Before serving stir well.

Linda Spindler   Knoxville, Tennessee

GREEK SALAD

1   can anchovy fillets, drained, save oil
    Olive oil
½   cup wine vinegar
1   bay leaf
1   clove garlic
1   tsp. oregano
¼   cup chopped parsley
1   bunch romaine, torn into bite-size pieces
½   head lettuce, torn into bite-size pieces
4   endive leaves
2   red onions, thinly sliced
2   tomatoes, quartered
1   cucumber, scored and sliced
½   green pepper, cut in strips
8 to 10 Greek olives
¼ to ½ pound feta cheese, crumbled
4   hard-cooked eggs, quartered

Combine reserved anchovy oil and olive oil to equal ½ cup.
In a jar combine oils, vinegar, bay leaf, garlic and oregano.
Shake well and chill several hours or overnight. In a large
salad bowl, combine parsley and remaining vegetables,
anchovy fillets and cheese. Before serving, remove bay leaf
and garlic from dressing; shake well and pour over salad.
Makes 4 to 6 servings.

Trina Kinsey   Averill Park, New York

SEVEN LAYER SALAD

1 (10 oz.) pkg. frozen peas
1 head iceberg lettuce, shredded
1 cup chopped celery
1 cup chopped green pepper

2 cups mayonnaise
3 T. graded Parmesan cheese
½ lb. sliced bacon, cooked and
crumbled

In medium saucepan cook peas as package label directs but for only one minute, then drain. In large glass salad bowl layer lettuce, celery, green pepper and peas. Spread mayonnaise evenly over top. Sprinkle on cheese and bacon. Cover and refrigerate 24 hours before serving. Do not toss at serving time; use large salad spoons to dip salad out in wedges.

Sheila Abert   San Diego, California

TACO SALAD

1 large red onion or 1 bunch small
green onions, diced
1 to 2 lbs. ground chuck
1 pkg. taco seasoning mix per lb.
of ground chuck
1 to 2 medium green peppers,
diced
1 head lettuce, shredded

2 to 3 large tomatoes, diced
1 can kidney beans, drained
½ lb. bag plain Doritos,
crushed
1 large pkg. cheddar cheese,
shredded

Brown meat, adding onion, taco seasoning and green pepper. Drain mixture and let stand till cool. In large salad bowl combine lettuce, tomatoes, kidney beans and meat mixture; toss. Top mixture with Doritos and cheese. Serve as a meal or side dish with MILD taco sauce or Italian dressing. Salad can be served with Doritos on the side instead of on top. Chips tend to become soggy if there are leftovers.

Mary Morris   Fairbanks, Alaska

SOUR CREAM CUCUMBERS

2 cucumbers, peeled and thinly
sliced
1 small onion, thinly sliced
½ cup white vinegar

salt and pepper to taste
2 T. sugar
8 oz. sour cream

Place cucumber and onions in shallow dish. Cover with vinegar, salt, pepper and sugar. Chill overnight. Next day, drain well and mix with sour cream. Chill.

Joyce Brown   Arlington, Texas

VEGETABLE SALAD

1 can French style beans, drained and chopped
1 jar pimento drained and finely chopped (2 oz. size)

1 can Petit Pois peas drained

MARINADE
¼ cup sugar
⅓ cup salad oil
¼ tsp. pepper

⅔ cup sugar
1 tsp. salt

Heat to boiling point and pour over the above canned vegetables. Let stand overnight.

NEXT DAY ADD
4 stems celery, finely diced
½ small green pepper, slivered
½ cup sharp cheddar cheese finely cubed

4 green onions, thinly sliced
4 cauliflower florets, finely chopped

Note: Use as a relish or drain and serve in lettuce cup as a salad.

Peg Novotny   Glendale, Missouri

HEAVENLY CHEESE MOLD

20 oz. crushed pineapple
6 oz. lemon gelatin
2 cups boiling water

1 cup mayonnaise
1 cup sharp Cheddar cheese, grated

Drain pineapple and reserve ¾ cup juice. Dissolve gelatin in water. Add juice. Gradually add mayonnaise. Mix well and chill until slightly thickened. Fold in pineapple and cheese. Pour into 1 ½ quart mold. Chill. Unmold on bed of lettuce. Serves 8.

Jill Laymond   Memphis, Tennessee

FRUIT SALAD

2 cups miniature marshmallows
1 can Mandarin oranges, drained
1 cup pineapple

1 cup coconut
1 cup sour cream

Mix and let stand overnight. Serves 6.

Jane Lunsford   Dayton, Ohio

SPINACH SALAD SUPREME

1 lb. fresh spinach	1 T. bacon drippings
6 strips bacon	1 cup mayonnaise
1 tsp. prepared mustard	¼ cup salad oil
½ tsp. sugar	¼ cup vinegar
1 small onion, grated	¼ cup Parmesan cheese

Wash spinach 3 times. Dry, tear and chill for several hours. Fry bacon, reserve drippings. Make dressing by beating all other ingredients together. When serving, toss spinach with dressing, top with bacon and additional cheese. Dressing keeps well.

Carole Macke   Dallas, Texas

CHRISTMAS SALAD

1 pkg. (14 oz.) marshmallows, cut up	2 cups Cool Whip
1 can (#2) pineapple, drain and save juice	1 lb. Tokay grapes, cut and seeded

Dressing:

2 eggs, beaten	¼ cup lemon juice
2 T. flour	1 cup sugar
¼ cup orange juice	½ cup pineapple juice

Cook dressing until thick. Cool. Blend Cool Whip, marshmallows, pineapple, grapes. Walnuts may be added if desired.

Shirley Parker   Boulder, Colorado

BANANA SPLIT SALAD

2 cups graham crackers, crushed	2 lbs. bananas
4 T. margarine, melted	1 can (large) crushed pineapple, drained
1 stick margarine	
2 eggs	2 pkg. Dream Whip
2 cups powdered sugar	

Add crushed graham crackers to melted margarine. Press in a 13x9 inch pan. Beat for 10 minutes margarine, eggs and powdered sugar. Spread over crackers. Split bananas and place on top of egg mixture. Place pineapple over the bananas. Spread with Dream Whip. If you desire nuts may be sprinkled over the top.

Evelyn Garrison   Santa Clara, California

PEACHES 'N' CHICKEN SALAD

½ cup sour cream
½ cup mayonnaise
½ tsp. rosemary
   dash of
   dash of sugar
   dash of pepper

2 cups chicken, cooked and
   cubed
1 cup sliced peaches, drained
   and diced
½ cup croutons
4 green pepper rings
   peach slices

Combine all ingredients except croutons, green peppers and peach slices. Toss and chill. Just before serving fold in croutons. Spoon onto pepper rings. Garnish with peach slices. Makes 4 servings.

Sandra Mc Farland   Cincinnati, Ohio

BING CHERRY SALAD
Serves 6

1 carton sour cream
½ cup sugar (or more to taste)

2 (3 oz.) packages cream
   cheese

Mix thoroughly until fluffy. Add: 1 can Bing cherries or black cherries (drained), 1 large can chunk or tidbit pineapple (drained), 1 heaping cup miniature marshmallows, ½ cup pecans. Refrigerate until ready to use.

Note: Save juices from fruit. Mix with 1 can frozen lemonade for a delicious punch that will serve 4.

Loretta Morris   Marshfield, Missouri

STRAWBERRY AND PRETZEL SALAD

2 cups pretzels (crushed not fine)
¾ cup margarine, melted
3 T. sugar
1 large pkg. strawberry Jello
2 cup boiling water

2 (10 oz.) pkg strawberries or
   2 cups fresh strawberries
1 (8 oz.) pkg. cream cheese
1 cup sugar
2 cups Cool Whip

Mix together pretzels, margarine and sugar. Press into 13x10 inch pan and bake at 400° for 8 to 10 minutes. Do not overbake. Mix jello, boiling water and strawberries; stir until dissolved. Place in refrigerator to cool for 30 minutes. Mix cream cheese and sugar; fold in Cool Whip. Spread over pretzel mixture; pour cooled jello on top and refrigerate. Let set 4 to 5 hours before serving. Can top with more Cool Whip.

Mable Anderson   Moline, Illinois

POTATO SALAD

5 lbs. potatoes
6 slices bacon, diced
¼ cup flour
4 cups water
6 T. sugar
1 T. salt
⅛ T. pepper
1 T. celery salt
¾ cup vinegar
½ cup chopped onion
6 hard-cooked eggs, sliced

Boil potatoes in their skins in salted water until tender. Peel while still warm. Cool. Slice into a large bowl. Fry bacon until crisp. Remove from pan; set aside. Stir flour into bacon fat and blend with a wooden spoon. Add water gradually, stirring until smooth and thick. Add sugar, salt, pepper, and celery salt; simmer and stir until dissolved. Add vinegar and bring to a boil, pour over the sliced potatoes. Add bacon pieces, onion, and sliced eggs; fold until well blended. When cool, cover and refrigerate.

Karen Hronek   Northbrook, Illinois

10 QUICK & EASY SALAD IDEAS

1. Combine fresh spinach, mandarin oranges, sliced red onions and creamy French dressing.
2. Toss lettuce, fresh cauliflower, olives, onions and blue cheese with oil and vinegar for a spicy salad.
3. Add thinly sliced, unpared, raw zucchini or broccoli stems and capers to green salad and dress with Italian dressing.
4. Mix a cup each of mayonnaise and sour cream with lemon-pepper seasoning to make a dressing for lettuce, tomatoes, grated cheese, chopped egg and croutons.
5. Stuff canned pears with a mixture of cream cheese, pear juice and pecans, and serve on lettuce.
6. Combine crabmeat, celery, mayonnaise, salt, pepper and grapefruit sections.
7. Make a salad of lettuce, tomatoes, avocados and sliced hard-boiled eggs tossed with Miracle Whip, salt and cracked pepper.
8. Make your own croutons from stale French bread sauteed in garlic butter, dried in a slow oven and stored in a glass jar.
9. Serve cold asparagus on a bed of lettuce topped with mayonnaise and lemon juice and garnished with pimento strips.
10. Frost grapes with slightly beaten egg white, sprinkle with sugar, and let dry on rack to use as a salad garnish.

Mae Meadows   Corpus Christi, Texas

Family Favorite

Salad
Notes

Ask the person whose card appears on the inside front cover of this book for a recipe form to submit your family favorite salads for next year's national cookbook.

Vegetables

PARTY POTATOES

32 oz. pkg. frozen hash browns,
slightly thawed
½ tsp. salt
¼ tsp. pepper
¼ cup onion, chopped

1 can Cream of Chicken soup
2 cups sour cream
1 cup grated Cheddar cheese
½ cup margarine
2 cups crushed Corn Flakes

Mix first seven ingredients together and place in a 3 quart casserole. Melt margarine and mix with Corn Flakes. Put mixture on top of casserole last 20 minutes of baking time. Bake total of 1 hour at 350 degrees.

Nellie C. Cain   Auxvasse, Missouri

BROCCOLI-CORN CASSEROLE

1 pkg. (10 oz.) frozen chopped
broccoli; thawed and well
drained
1 can creamed corn
2 T. chopped onion
¼ cup chopped green pepper

1 can (4 oz.) sliced
mushrooms; drained
2 eggs
1 stick butter or margarine;
melted
1½ cups stuffing crumbs

Put ½ cup of stuffing crumbs in a 1½ quart buttered baking dish. Mix melted butter with remaining crumbs and set aside. Combine remaining ingredients and put in baking dish, top with reserved crumbs. Bake at 350° for 1 hour. Serves 4 to 6.

Judy Bledsal   Evansville, Indiana

SPINACH ALMOND

1 pkg. (10 oz.) frozen spinach
1 can (8 oz.) mushrooms
1 pkg. (2½ oz.) slivered almonds

3 T. butter
salt and pepper to taste

Cook spinach according to package directions. Drain mushrooms and saute in butter. Combine spinach and mushrooms. Sprinkle with almonds. Serve hot. Makes 4 servings.

Nancy E. Walker   Minneapolis, Minnesota

POTATO CASSEROLE

2 lbs. hash browns
1 can chicken soup
2 cups Velvetta cheese
1 pint Half & Half

½ cup melted margarine
2 T. minced onion
1 tsp. salt
½ tsp. pepper

Combine all ingredients together in a 9x13 inch pan and bake 1 hour at 350°. Serves 8.

Elaine Cole   Augusta, Georgia

BROCCOLI-CHEESE DELIGHT

2 pkgs. (10 oz.) frozen chopped
   broccoli
½ cup chopped onion
2½ stalks celery, chopped
1 small can mushrooms
½ cup margarine
4 T. flour

2 cups milk
1 pkg. (8 oz.) cream cheese
4 oz. sharp cheddar cheese,
   shredded
½ cup bread crumbs
salt and pepper to taste

Saute onion and celery in margarine. Cook broccoli until tender in a small amount of water; drain. Add mushrooms, onion and celery to broccoli. In a saucepan melt 4 T. margarine; blend in flour, salt and pepper. Add milk, cook and stir until thick and bubbly. Reduce heat, blend in cream cheese until smooth. Pour half of sauce mixture on broccoli, then pour into a greased 9x13 inch casserole. Pour remaining sauce mixture over broccoli; sprinkle shredded cheese and bread crumbs on top. Cover and bake at 350° for 30 minutes. Makes 8 servings.

Sylvia Richards   Foxboro, Massachusetts

CREAMED ASPARAGUS

20 oz. frozen asparagus
¾ cup sour cream
½ cup Parmesan cheese
2 tsps. lemon juice

1 tsp. salt
½ cup sliced almonds, toasted
Dash of paprika

Cook asparagus and drain. Combine sour cream, cheese, lemon juice and salt in a saucepan. Heat slowly, but do not boil. Arrange asparagus on a platter. Top with cream sauce. Sprinkle paprika and almonds as a garnish.

Eleanor Black   Dallas, Texas

DELUXE GREEN BEANS

3 cups sliced fresh or frozen green beans
2 T. margarine or butter
⅓ cup chopped onion
2 T. whole wheat flour
½ T. salt
   Freshly ground black pepper to taste
1 cup dairy sour cream
½ cup grated Cheddar cheese

Steam beans until tender (about 10 min.). Preheat oven to 350°. Melt butter in a small, heavy-bottomed pan; add onion and sauté until tender. Stir in flour, salt, and pepper. When thoroughly mixed, add the sour cream very carefully and heat. Do not boil. Taste and correct seasonings. Stir sour cream mixture into hot beans; pour beans into greased 1-quart casserole. Top with cheese. Bake about 15 minutes or until cheese melts and beans are heated thoroughly. Serves 6.

Alice Meyer   Davenport, Iowa

CURT'S STUFFED TOMATOES

6 medium tomatoes	1 tsp. salt
½ cup chopped green pepper	garlic salt to taste
¼ cup grated parmesan or Romano cheese	onion salt to taste
	paprika
⅓ cup croutons (more croutons may be added for thickness)	sliced fresh mushrooms (optional)

Remove stem end from tomato, cut bottom flat. Clean out pulp (leaving ½ inch wall) and combine with all of the ingredients. Stuff tomatoes with this mixture. In an ungreased pan bake in 350° oven until tomato is heated through. Garnish with parsley and bacon.

Curt Hansen   New Berlin, Wisconsin

CARROT CASSEROLE

6 medium carrots	Salt and pepper to taste
2 medium onions, chopped	⅓ cup bread crumbs
4 T. butter	⅓ cup American cheese, grated
10¾ oz. condensed cream of mushroom soup	

Preheat oven to 350°. Wash and peel carrots. Boil in salted water until tender. Saute onions in butter until golden. Place carrots in greased 1 quart baking dish and mash. Add onions and soup. Blend well, adding salt and pepper. Sprinkle with bread crumbs and cheese. Bake until bubbly 25 minutes.

Rita Page   Austin, Texas

OLD FASHIONED BAKED BEANS

2 cups dried navy beans	½ cup dark Karo syrup
½ tsp. baking soda	½ cup ketchup
½ cup brown sugar	2 T. butter or margarine

Cook beans in salted water until tender but firm. Last few minutes of cooking time add the baking soda. Remove from heat and let set a few minutes. Drain off liquid, rinse with clear water. Put beans in baking dish. Add brown sugar, Karo syrup, ketchup and butter. Cover with bacon strips. Bake uncovered at 350° until brown, about 1 hour. (If a sweeter taste is desired add additional brown sugar.) Makes 6 servings.

Jeannie Clark   San Francisco, California

GREEN BEAN CASSEROLE

¼ cup butter
9 oz. pkg. frozen French style
   green beans, thawed, drained
¾ tsp. Italian herb seasoning*
¼ tsp. garlic salt

2 oz. jar chopped pimiento,
   undrained
14 oz. can artichoke hearts,
   drained, cut into squares
½ cup chopped pecans

In 2-qt. saucepan melt butter over medium heat. Stir in all ingredients except artichokes and pecans. Cover; cook, stirring occasionally, until green beans are crisply tender (5 to 7 min.). Stir in artichokes and pecans. Cover; continue cooking until artichokes are heated through (2 to 3 min.). Serves 4.

* ¼ tsp. each oregano leaves, marjoram leaves, basil leaves and ⅛ tsp. sage can be substituted for ¾ tsp. Italian herb seasoning.

Kathryn Barnes   Washington, D.C.

CORN PUDDING

2 (1 lb.) cans creamed corn
3 eggs
2 T. flour
⅓ cup sugar

2 tsps. salt
1 cup cream (half and half is
   fine)

Combine the above. Pour in baking dish. Dot with butter and bake at 350 degrees for 45 minutes or until lightly browned.

Donna Fredricks   Albuquerque, New Mexico

GREEN BEANS VINAIGRETTE

2 (16 oz.) cans French style
   green beans
1 T. chopped onion
½ cup French dressing
6 hard cooked eggs, chopped
½ cup ripe olives, chopped

⅓ cup dairy sour cream
1 T. vinegar
½ tsp. prepared mustard
   salt
6 slices crisp bacon, crumbled

Drain beans; place in shallow baking dish. Sprinkle with onion. Add dressing and turn to coat beans well. Marinate at least two hours. Mix eggs, olives, cream, vinegar and mustard. Add salt to taste. At serving time arrange beans on platter. Top with egg mixture. Garnish with bacon. Makes 8 servings.

Carlene Baumheuter   Cahokia, Illinois

FRESH VEGETABLES AND DIP

1 stalk celery, cut into 2″ pieces
2 green peppers, julienned
3 carrots, julienned
1 small head cauliflower, broken into flowerets
8 cherry tomatoes
8 scallions, washed and trimmed
8 mushrooms, wiped clean
½ cup vegetable oil
½ cup butter
2 cloves garlic, minced
6 anchovies, minced

Wash all vegetables and place in a large bowl with ice. Refrigerate until needed. Place oil, butter, garlic, pepper and anchovies in top of a double boiler and heat thoroughly. Cover and reduce heat. Simmer for 15 min. Arrange vegetables on a platter. Pour heated butter mixture into a bowl and serve. Serves 4 to 6.

Kris Durham   Norton Shores, Michigan

50

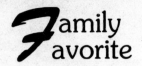

Family Favorite

Vegetable Notes

Ask the person whose card appears on the inside front cover of this book for a recipe form to submit your family favorite vegetables for next year's national cookbook.

Meats

FESTIVE PORK ROAST

¾ cup dry red wine	1 clove garlic, minced
⅓ cup packed brown sugar	1 tsp. curry powder
¼ cup vinegar	½ tsp. ground ginger
¼ cup catsup	¼ tsp. pepper
¼ cup water	1 5-lb. boneless rolled pork
2 T. cooking oil	roast
1 T. soy sauce	1 tsp. cornstarch

Combine wine, brown sugar, vinegar, catsup, water, cooking oil, soy sauce, garlic, curry powder, ginger, and pepper. Place meat in plastic bag; set in shallow dish. Pour marinade over meat; close bag. Marinate in refrigerator 6 to 8 hours or overnight, turning several times. Drain meat, reserving 1 ¼ cups marinade. Pat meat dry with paper toweling. Place meat on rack in shallow roasting pan. Roast in 325° oven for 2 ¼ to 3 ¾ hours or till meat thermometer registers 170°. Blend cornstarch and reserved marinade; cool and stir till thickened and bubbly. Brush roast often with marinade during last 15 min. of cooking. Reheat remaining sauce and pass with meat.

Karen Cruz   Bloomington, Indiana

HAMBURGER STROGANOFF

4 (6 oz.) cans sliced mushrooms, drained	4 tsp. salt
	1 tsp. pepper
3 cups chopped onions	¼ cup red vinegar
4 cloves garlic, minced	¼ cup flour
½ cup butter or margarine	1 can Pet Milk, soured with
4 lbs. ground beef	vinegar (1 T. vinegar)
4 cans (10½ oz.) Cream of	1 pkg. (28 oz.) noodles,
Chicken Soup	cooked and drained

Cook onions and mushrooms until tender. Add meat and cook until brown. Mix soup, flour, salt and pepper to meat mixture. Bring to boil then simmer for 10 minutes. Add soured milk and noodles. Heat through and serve.

Bonnie Graham   Waynesville, Missouri

KIBBIE

2	cups cracked wheat	½	tsp. pepper
1	small onion, grated	1	T. salt
2	lbs. very lean ground round beef	1	T. ground allspice
		1	tsp. sweet basil

Wash and drain wheat; refrigerate for 30 minutes. Grate onion into meat and add spices. Remove wheat from refrigerator and cover with ice water or ice. Squeeze the water out of the wheat and add by handfuls to the meat. When well mixed, sprinkle with a little ice water to soften and lightly knead. Taste for seasonings. Kibbie may be eaten raw, fried or baked. To fry, shape into patties and deep fry in corn oil. Serves 12.

Ann Kallail   Cedar Rapids, Iowa

ROAST TENDERLOIN DIANE

¼	cup dry white wine	1	tsp. worcestershire sauce
¼	cup brandy	¼	tsp. freshly ground pepper
3	T. lemon juice	1	2-lb beef tenderloin
2	T. snipped chives	2	T. water
1½	tsp. salt	2	T. butter or margarine

Combine wine, brandy, lemon juice, chives, salt, worcestershire, and pepper. Place meat in plastic bag; set in loaf dish. Pour marinade over meat and tie bag closed. Let stand no longer than 2 hours at room temperature or overnight in refrigerator, occasionally pressing bag against meat to distribute marinade. Remove meat, reserving marinade. Pat meat dry with paper toweling. Place tenderloin on rack in shallow roasting pan. Bake in 425° oven for 45 to 55 min., basting the meat occasionally with about half of the marinade. In small saucepan heat remaining marinade, the water, and butter or margarine till mixture bubbles. Slice meat and arrange on heated platter. Spoon sauce over meat. Garnish with cooked mushroom halves, if desired. Serves 6.

Connie Reid   Carbondale, Illinois

MEATLOAF

2	lbs. beef or meatloaf mix	2	eggs
¾	to 1 cup quick Quaker Oats	1	pkg. dry Onion soup mix
½	cup small curd Cottage cheese	½	to ¾ cup water

Mix all ingredients together and place in loaf pan. Bake at 350° for 1 hour.

Brenda Ribaudo   Algonquin, Illinois

HAMBURGER POPS

1 lb. ground beef	¼ tsp. pepper
¼ cup fine bread crumbs	3 T. milk
1 T. grated onion	1 dill pickle
½ tsp. salt	

Cut pickle lengthwise into 6 strips. Mix together all ingredients except pickle. Divide meat mixture into 6 portions. Shape meat around pickle into rolls. Broil. Insert wooden skewers in center. Or, if desired, omit skewer and serve on long buns.

Lois Kane   Brainerd, Minnesota

REUBEN PIE

1 egg, beaten	1 8 oz. can sauerkraut,
⅓ cup evaporated milk	drained and snipped
¾ cup rye bread crumbs	12 oz. corned beef, chopped
¼ cup chopped onion	(1 ½ cups thinly sliced)
¼ tsp. salt	Pie pastry for 1 deep-dish
Dash pepper	pie crust
	6 oz. Swiss cheese, grated

In mixing bowl combine first 7 ingredients. Add chuck, sauerkraut and corned beef. Mix well. Place ½ of meat mixture into pastry shell and sprinkle with ½ of cheese. Cover with remaining meat mixture. Top with cheese and bake at 400°F for 25-30 minutes. Serves 6.

Helen Hoos   Rock Island, Illinois

BRAISED SHOULDER OF LAMB

1 5 lb. shoulder of lamb	12 small onions
Garlic cloves, slivered	2 tsps. salt
5 T. olive oil	¾ tsp. each thyme, pepper
6 tomatoes, peeled, halved and	Chopped fresh parsley
seeded	Lemon juice

Bone and roll lamb and stud with garlic. In Dutch oven brown meat well on all sides in olive oil. Add vegetables and seasonings. Cover the pot and simmer the meat slowly 1 ½ hours. Transfer the lamb to a heated platter; arrange the vegetables around it. Bring sauce to a boil; reduce it over high heat for 4-5 minutes. Pour over lamb and vegetables. Sprinkle lavishly with chopped parsley and lemon juice.

Mrs. William French   Dayton, Ohio

BEEF KABOBS

½ cup vegetable oil
1 tsp. salt
¼ tsp. pepper
½ tsp. oregano
½ tsp. garlic powder
1½ lbs. round steak, cut into cubes
12 cherry tomatoes
12 fresh mushrooms, cleaned
2 medium onions, cut in eighths
2 green peppers, cut into large pieces

Combine oil, salt, pepper, oregano and garlic powder in a large bowl. Mix thoroughly. Add beef cubes and mix lightly. Cover and allow steak to marinate for ninety minutes. Place steak alternately on skewers with tomatoes, mushrooms, onions and green peppers, ending with tomato. Place skewers on a flat baking sheet and broil until meat is the desired degree of doneness. Serve over rice. Serves 4.

Barbara Lee   Plano, Texas

KOREAN STEAK

1 lb. round steak cut up	season to taste
1 bunch green onions, sliced	¼ green pepper, sliced
3 T. soy sauce	3 T. salad oil
2 T. sugar	1 clove garlic

Mix all ingredients and pour over steak; place in baking dish and refrigerate and marinate overnight. When marinate reaches room temperature, broil 8 minutes or until done, turning once.

Sandy Stevens   Barr, Illinois

LAMB MIXED GRILL
Makes 2 to 3 servings

1 lb. boneless lamb, cut into 1½ inch cubes	2 T. Dijon mustard
2 T. olive oil	2 garlic cloves, crushed
salt and pepper to taste	6 small whole onions, peeled and halved
3 medium potatoes, peeled and halved	6 medium mushrooms
8 cherry tomatoes	4 T. salad oil

Pre-cook onions and potatoes. Thread lamb cubes on metal skewers. Combine mustard, oil, one clove of garlic, crushed, and brush on all sides of meat. Sprinkle with salt and pepper; arrange kabobs on greased grill over moderate coals. Cook, turn and baste for 15 minutes; thread vegetables on skewers. Add salad oil and remaining crushed garlic to mustard basting mixture; brush on all vegetables. Grill with lamb kabobs for 5 to 10 minutes or until meat is pink and vegetables are hot; turn and baste frequently.

Chef Gus Pavlakis   Florissant, Missouri

STEAK

1 thick fillet steak	1 T. Cognac
salt and pepper	2 T. whipping cream
2 T. butter	1 tsp. prepared mustard

Season steak with salt and pepper and sear on both sides in hot butter in frying pan. Remove and keep hot. Rinse pan with Cognac; add cream. Stir well and reduce liquid by half. Just before serving add mustard. Stir well and pour over steak. One serving.

May Madson   Atlanta, Georgia

PORK N' POTATO MAIN DISH
Serves 6

6 pork steaks, bone in or boneless
American or Velveeta cheese
(as much as desired)

6 medium potatoes, peeled and
sliced
2 cans cream of mushroom
soup

Brown pork steaks in skillet; place in bottom of 13x9 inch baking dish (steaks can overlap each other). Place potato slices evenly over meat; put cheese over potatoes. Pour cream of mushroom soup over top of cheese. Bake in moderate oven for approximately 1 hour or until meat and potatoes are tender.

Kathy Collins   Oblong, Illinois

BEEF DISH

1 can celery soup
1 can mushroom soup
1 pkg. onion soup mix

2 lbs. stew meat (don't brown
meat)
¾ cup white sherry wine

Mix all ingredients together. Bake in deep casserole dish for 3 hours in 300° oven. Serve over rice or noodles.

Beverly Barnett   Mission Viejo, California

BEEF STEW

4 to 6 medium carrots,
scrubbed and scraped
6 to 8 medium potatoes
3 T. cooking oil
2½ to 3 cups water

2 to 3 medium onions
1½ to 2 lbs. boneless beef
(chuck or round), cut up in
1 inch cubes

Place cooking oil in a 3 quart pan over low heat. Add onions and cook until light brown. Add beef and brown on all sides. Bring water to a boil and add carrots cut in strips. Cook 10 to 15 minutes. Add potatoes; cover and let simmer 20 minutes. Add remaining onions and simmer 15 minutes.

MIX A PASTE OF:
¼ cup flour and ¾ cup water

Add some broth and add to stew slowly. Simmer until gravy is thickened. Season to taste. Note: Serve over hot biscuits or Texas bread.

Kathryn Clifford   Fort Worth, Texas

KENTUCKY BURGOO

2 lbs. chicken	2 cups carrots
2 lbs. pork	2 cups corn
2 lbs. beef	corn starch
2 cups green beans	salt

Defat and debone meats. Place in slow cooker on medium, cover to top of meat with water, and cook 20 to 24 hours. Add 4 cups boiling water. Thicken with corn starch until light gravy. Add vegetables and cook until tender. Add salt to taste.

J.L. Thomas   Lexington, Kentucky

CHEESEBURGER IMPOSSIBLE PIE

1 lb. hamburger	½ tsp. salt
½ cup chopped onion	dash of pepper
1 ½ cups milk	1 cup grated cheese (cheddar)
3 eggs	¾ cup Bisquick

Brown meat and onion, drain; place in greased 10 inch pie plate; cover with cheese; sprinkle with salt and pepper. Blend milk, eggs and Bisquick in blender for 30 seconds and pour over cheese and meat. Bake at 350° F. for 30 minutes.

Amelia Harter   Brookview, New York

ORIENTAL BEEF AND PORK DINNER
Serves 8 people

1 lb. beef, diced (un-cooked)	1 lb. pork, diced (un-cooked)
6 T. soy sauce	1 cup water
1 large bunch of celery cut in	1 large onion, chopped
½ inch pieces	¼ cup water
2 T. cornstarch	1 2 oz. can mushrooms
1 10½ oz. can water chestnuts, drained	1 10½ oz. can bamboo shoots, drained
salt and pepper to taste	

Brown meat in hot fat or grease. Drain excess fat. Add soy sauce and cup of water. Simmer for 2 minutes. Add celery and onion. Simmer 1 ½ hours. Blend cornstarch and ¼ cup water. Stir into mixture until smooth. Add water chestnuts, bean sprouts and bamboo shoots. Heat through. Season with salt and pepper. Serve over dry noodles, rice or toast.

Norma Snow   Bridgeton, Missouri

MARINATED BEEF SHORT RIBS

2 quarts cider vinegar or red wine
2 quarts water
½ cup brown sugar
2 T. dry mustard
6 whole cloves
2 sticks cinnamon
3 T. pickling spice
1 T. ground ginger
2 T. pepper
4 or 5 lbs. lean beef short ribs

Combine first 10 ingredients and simmer 30-40 minutes. Allow to cool. Pour marinade over short ribs which have been seasoned with additional salt and pepper and marinate 24 hours in refrigerator. Cook about 4-5 hours on covered grill. Do not place meat directly over fire.

Thelma Warren   Corpus Cristi, Texas

VEAL MARSALA

8 veal medallions, sliced in thin strips
¼ cup oil or melted margarine
1 4 oz. can sliced mushrooms, drained or fresh, sliced
¼ cup chopped onion
2 green peppers, sliced in thin strips
½ tsp. celery salt
¼ tsp. black pepper
½ tsp. Italian seasoning
½ cup Marsala wine

Saute veal in oil. Add vegetables and seasonings. Cook over low heat until tender. Add wine and simmer 3-4 minutes. Serves 4.

June Mueller   Fort Worth, Texas

SOUTHERN COMFORT GRILLED CHUCK ROAST

2 ½ to 3 lb. chuck roast, sprinkled with unseasoned tenderizer and left to stand overnight in the refrigerator
¼ cup Southern Comfort Bourbon (or any bourbon)
¾ bottle soy sauce (small size)
1 ½ cups water
⅓ cup brown sugar
1 tsp. lemon juice

Mix all marinade ingredients thoroughly. Place meat in a deep dish or pan and pour the mixture over it. Marinate for 5 to 6 hours turning every 30 minutes. Cook on charcoal grill or on high on gas grill for 30 to 60 minutes, depending on how well done you like it. It can also be cooked in the oven at 400° for about 40 minutes. Slice and serve. Serves 6 to 8.

Georgie M. Booker   Atlanta, Georgia

61

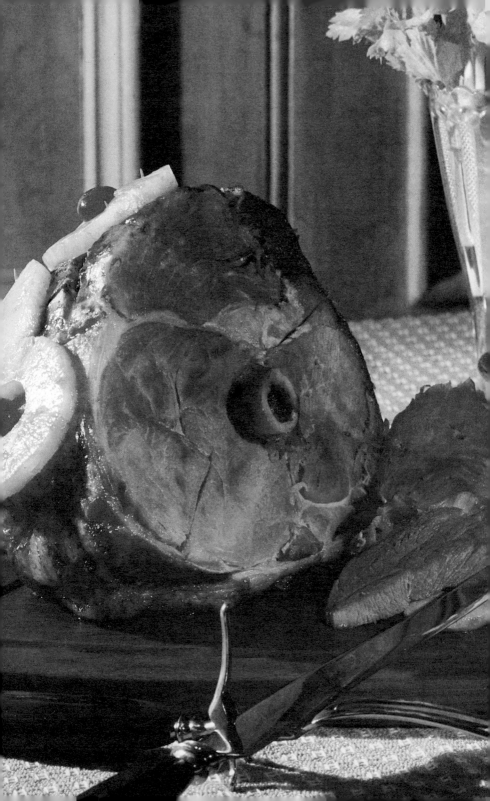

WESTERN HAM

5 to 10-lb. country ham (with bone)
10 to 12 whole cloves
1 12-oz. can pineapple slices
6 to 8 maraschino cherries
  Pineapple Glaze

With a sharp knife, remove as much skin and fat as possible from ham. Puncture at intervals with an ice pick and insert whole cloves. Barbecue ham over medium indirect heat for 2 ¼ to 3 hours. Baste with Pineapple Glaze every 15 minutes the last hour of cooking. Remove cloves. Place pineapple slices with cherry centers on top of ham. Secure with toothpicks. Baste once. Close cover and barbecue for 20 minutes.

Nicki Weld   Tustin, California

PINEAPPLE GLAZE

1 cup pineapple juice or juice from
  pineapple slices or chunks
½ cup cider vinegar
¼ cup black molasses
2 T. maraschino cherry juice
1 T. brown sugar
1 T. cornstarch

Combine pineapple juice, vinegar, molasses, cherry juice, and brown sugar in saucepan. Mix well. Blend in cornstarch. Cook over low heat, stirring constantly until thickened. Makes 1 ½ cups.

amily Favorite

Meat

Notes

Ask the person whose card appears on the inside front cover of this book for a recipe form to submit your family favorite meats for next year's national cookbook.

Poultry

OVEN-FRIED HERBED CHICKEN

6 chicken breasts, halved
1 cup crumbled herb-seasoned
   croutons
⅔ cup grated Parmesan cheese

¼ cup fresh or 2 T. dried
   parsley
½ cup butter, melted
Garlic powder to taste

Combine croutons, parsley and garlic powder in a mixing bowl. Mix thoroughly. Dip chicken first in melted butter then in crumb mixture to coat well. Place in buttered shallow baking dish. Pour remaining butter over chicken. Top with remaining crumbs. Bake, uncovered at 325° 1 ¼ hours. Do not turn. Serves 4 to 6.

Barbara E. Dickey   Dunedin, Florida

CHICKEN SALAD

2 cups cooked chicken, diced
½ tsp. salt
½ cup nuts, chopped
2 T. lemon juice
½ cup cheddar cheese, grated

2 cups celery, diced
1 T. onion, minced
1 cup mayonnaise
½ cup stuffed olives, sliced
1 cup potato chips, crushed

Combine all ingredients except cheese and potato chips. Spoon into buttered 1 ½ qt. casserole. Combine cheese and potato chips and sprinkle over chicken mixture. Bake in 375° F. oven for 20 minutes. Serve hot. Serves 6-8.

Carol Strickland   Odessa, Texas

DRESSED UP CHICKEN

1 4 lb. chicken, cup up
1 10 oz. jar apricot jelly or
   preserves
1 pkg. onion soup mix

1 8 oz. bottle Russian or 1000
   Island dressing
   butter

Place chicken in buttered casserole dish. Mix dressing, jelly and onion soup mix together. Spread over the chicken. Bake in pre-heated oven for 1 hr. at 350° F. Serves 6-8.

Janice S. McKenzie Harvey   Villa Ridge, Missouri

BEER BATTER CHICKEN

1 3½-lb. fryer, cut in serving pieces
1 stalk celery, sliced
1 small onion, sliced
1 carrot, sliced
1 tsp. salt
¼ tsp. pepper
Beer Batter
Vegetable oil
Flour

Place chicken pieces in a heavy kettle and cover with water. Add celery, onion, and carrot. Season with salt and pepper, and simmer until tender, about 20 to 25 minutes. Cool meat. Shake chicken pieces in flour, then dip in Beer Batter, and deep fry in 375° oil about 5 minutes.

BEER BATTER

3 eggs
½ cup flour
½ cup cornstarch
¼ tsp. curry powder
½ tsp. sugar
1 tsp. seasoned salt
⅓ cup beer or water

Beat eggs. Add ½ cup flour, cornstarch, curry powder, sugar, salt, beer or water and blend well.

Ana Eisenhart   South Bend, Indiana

66

CHICKEN FRITTERS

1 ⅓ cups sifted flour
½ tsp. baking powder
1 tsp. salt
2 eggs, beaten

⅔ cup milk
1 T. salad oil
4 large chicken breast halves

Cut chicken off bone and cut into pieces about 1 inch square. (Chicken will cut easier if partially frozen.) Set aside. Mix together dry ingredients and liquids in separate bowls. Roll chicken in liquid; then in dry ingredients. Deep fry in hot oil until puffy and golden, about 6-10 minutes, turning once. Drain on paper towels. Serve at once. Makes 4 servings.

Linda L. Struemph   Jefferson City, Missouri

SAFFRON BROILED CHICKEN

2 small broiling chickens,
   quartered
   salt and pepper to taste

¼ tsp. saffron
   juice of 1 lemon

Preheat broiler. Put chicken pieces, skin side down, on foil-covered baking sheet (this makes cleanup easier). Sprinkle lightly with salt and pepper, ½ the saffron, and ½ the lemon juice. Broil for 8 to 10 minutes, until crispy and golden brown. Turn chicken pieces. Season with salt, pepper and remaining saffron and lemon juice. Broil for another 8 to 10 minutes, adjusting heat if necessary so skin turns crispy and golden. Serve hot or warm.

Julie Anderson   Silvis, Illinois

TURKEY QUICHE

1 9 inch pie crust, unbaked
1 cup chopped, cooked turkey
2 T. chopped green onions
1 3 oz. pkg. cream cheese,
   softened
2 T. dry vermouth

4 eggs
1 cup heavy cream
½ cup milk
½ tsp. salt
¼ tsp. crushed rosemary

Mix turkey with onion, cream cheese, and vermouth; spread in crust. Beat eggs with heavy cream, add milk, and seasonings, and pour over turkey mixture. Bake at 450° for 10 minutes. Reduce temperature to 350° and bake for 40 more minutes.

Janet Wagner   Oklahoma City, Oklahoma

SHRIMPLY CHICK-ENCHANTING

1 pint sour cream
1 envelope gravy mix for chicken
¼ tsp. salt
6 chicken breast halves
¾ cup cornflake crumbs

¼ cup butter or margarine
1 cup cooked or canned
   shrimp, coarsely chopped
¼ cup chopped ripe olives
2 T. diced pimentos

Combine sour cream, gravy mix and salt. Divide in half and refrigerate one-half. Coat chicken with remaining sour cream mixture. Roll in crumbs. Melt butter in shallow baking pan; arrange chicken skin side down in pan. Bake at 350° for 45 minutes. Turn, and bake 20 minutes longer or until tender and brown. Add shrimp, olives and pimentos to refrigerated sour cream, heat slowly, do not boil. Serve over chicken. Serves 6.

Sally Lewis   Silver Spring, Maryland

CRUSTY BAKED CHICKEN

3 full chicken breasts or 1 whole
   chicken
   salt
   pepper

1 pint sour cream
1 small package Pepperidge
   Farm dressing
   butter

Season chicken breasts with salt and pepper to taste. Lay in a shallow baking dish. Spread thickly with sour cream, sprinkle thickly with poultry dressing and dot well with butter. Bake at 350° for about 40 minutes or until crisp and tender. This may be prepared well ahead of time and refrigerated until ready to cook. Makes 4-6 servings.

Doris Farina   St Paul, Minnesota

CHICKEN CASSEROLE

1 can condensed cream of chicken
   soup
1 soup can of water
1 soup can (1⅓ cups) minute rice,
   uncooked

1 can condensed cream of
   celery soup
1 can (12 oz.) boned chicken
1 can (3½ oz.) french fried
   onions

Combine soups, water and chicken; add rice. Stir to mix. Bring quickly to a boil. Cover; reduce heat. Simmer for 7 minutes; stir occasionally. Top with heated onions. Serves 4-6.

Dorothy Herman   Tulsa, Oklahoma

CREOLE FOR 6 WITH RICE

4 cups canned tomatoes, coarsely chopped and drained
2 cups onion, coarsely chopped
1 cup green pepper, coarsely chopped
1 cup celery, coarsely chopped
2 tsps. garlic, finely chopped
½ tsp. cayenne pepper

2 T. cornstarch mixed with ¼ cup water
4 lbs. chicken, cut-up
1 cup water
½ cup oil
2 bay leaves
1 T. paprika
1 T. salt

Heat oil over moderate heat. Add onion, green pepper, celery and garlic; cook for 5 minutes, stir frequently. Stir in tomatoes, water, bay leaves, paprika, cayenne pepper and salt. Bring to a boil over high heat, add chicken and reduce heat to a simmer. Cover and cook for 35 minutes; stir in cornstarch and water. Cook for 3 minutes; serve over rice.

Note: Suggest Uncle Ben's Rice (converted) for 6 people.

Scott Higgins   Sturgeon Bay, Wisconsin

BATTER FRIED CHICKEN

2 2½ lbs. chicken, cut up
1 cup flour
2 tsps. salt
½ tsp. pepper

½ tsp. baking soda
1 cup buttermilk
Cooking oil to fill deep fryer

Preheat deep fat fryer to 350°. Shake each piece of chicken separately in a paper bag containing flour, salt and pepper. Add soda to buttermilk. Dip chicken in mixture and the back into flour mixture. Cook in deep fat 20-25 minutes. Drain on absorbent paper.

Elizabeth Milton   Chattanooga, Tennessee

TURKEY BRUNCH FOR SIX

1 cup turkey, cooked and diced
1 cup Cheddar cheese
1 egg, beaten well
6 T. mayonnaise

Dash Tabasco sauce
Pinch of salt
3 English muffins, split

Mix turkey, cheese, egg, mayonnaise, Tabasco sauce, and salt together. Place mixture on muffins and bake in a 375° oven for 8-10 minutes or until lightly browned and puffy.

Sharon Dalaney   San Antonio, Texas

CHICKEN PARISIENNE

12 small chicken breasts, skinned and boned
16 oz. currant jelly
1 T. cornstarch
1 cup water
¼ cup fresh lemon juice
2 tsps. ground allspice
2 T. Worcestershire
3 tsps. salt
1 tsp. pepper

Preheat oven to 450° F. Place chicken breasts in uncovered roasting pan, large enough so that they do not overlap. Mix all other ingredients in a saucepan and bring to a boil. Simmer 5 minutes. Pour sauce over the chicken breasts and bake for 15 minutes. Reduce heat to 350° and bake 30 minutes, basting frequently. Serve with rice.

Lorraine Brooks
Indianapolis, Indiana

DUCK WITH SAUERKRAUT

1 4-5 lb. duck
4 cups sauerkraut
4 carrots, thinly sliced
2 stalks celery, diced
1 medium onion, diced
2 potatoes, diced
2 tomatoes, diced
3 T. sugar
½ tsp. caraway seed
1 cup apple cider
1 tsp. seasoned salt
1 cup sour cream

Place duck in roasting pan. Mix remaining ingredients together, except sour cream, and stuff duck lightly. Place any remaining mixture around duck and cover. Bake in a 350° oven for 2 ½ hours or until tender. Skim off fat. Add 1 cup sour cream to vegetable mixture.

Margaret Rose
Rock Island, Illinois

CHICKEN SUPREME

1 chicken, cut in parts
3 T. fresh grated ginger root
1 lemon, sliced
1 tsp. salt
1 tsp. Accent
½ tsp. ground mace
¼ tsp. curry powder
¼ tsp. pepper
¼ cup corn oil
¼ cup water

Place chicken in shallow baking pan in single layer, skin side up. Sprinkle over all ginger root, lemon, salt, Accent, mace, curry powder and pepper. Pour over corn oil and water. Bake in 350° F oven, covered, ½ hour. Remove cover and add more water, if necessary. Continue baking until chicken is browned about ½ hour. Serve with rice.

Carole Harrison
Augusta, Georgia

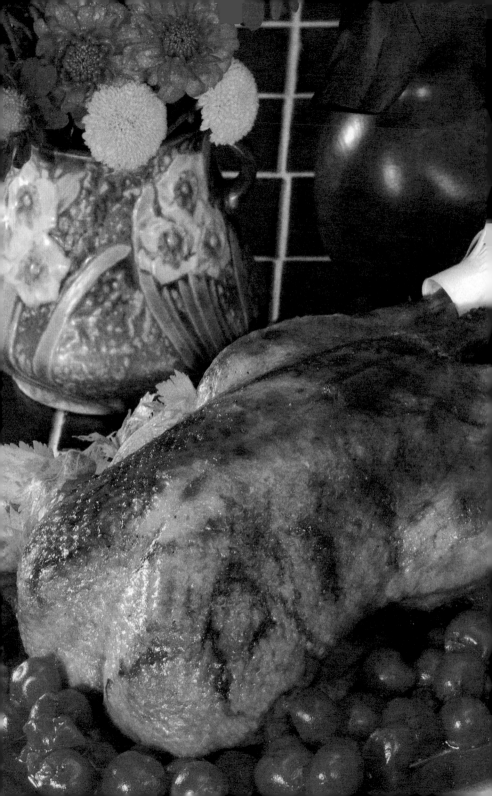

ROAST DUCK WITH CHERRIES

1 5-lb. duck
  salt and pepper or seasoned salt
1 stalk celery, chopped
1 onion, chopped
1 carrot, chopped
1 cup red wine
1 cup orange juice
1 16-oz. can pitted bing cherries, drained
2 T. cornstarch mixed with
  2 T. water

Season duck inside and out with salt and pepper or seasoned salt, and place in roasting pan. Arrange celery, onion, and carrot pieces around duck. Cover and bake for 2 to 2½ hours in a 350° oven. The last half hour, pour off drippings, remove vegetables, and add wine and orange juice; do not cover. When done, add cherries and mix well. Remove duck to a platter and bring drippings to a boil. Add cornstarch mixture. Simmer for 2 to 3 minutes. Pour over duck. Serves 2 to 4.

Rebecca Foster   Tempe, Arizona

Family Favorite

Poultry Notes

Ask the person whose card appears on the inside front cover of this book for a recipe form to submit your family favorite poultry for next year's national cookbook.

Fish and Seafood

SHRIMP SLAW

4 cups thin-sliced red or green
  cabbage (about 1 pound)
1 medium-sized zucchini, cut into
  matchstick-size pieces
1 10-oz. pkg. frozen corn kernels
  (about 2 cups), rinsed with hot
  water to thaw
4 T. butter or margarine
½ cup thin-sliced scallions
1 4-oz. can chopped green
  chilies, drained

2 tsps. minced fresh garlic
1¼ pounds uncooked large
  shrimp, peeled
1 cup buttermilk
1 cup heavy cream
2 T. Worcestershire sauce
½ tsp. salt
⅛ tsp. pepper

Mix cabbage, zucchini and corn in a bowl. Melt butter in a 10 to 12 inch skillet over moderate heat. Add scallions, chilies and garlic and cook 2 min., or until scallions begin to soften. Add shrimp and cook 2 to 3 min., just until shrimp turn pink; do not overcook. Spoon shrimp over cabbage mixture. Add remaining ingredients to skillet and increase heat to high. Boil 7 to 10 minutes, stirring occasionally, until sauce is reduced to about 1⅓ cups. Pour sauce over shrimp and toss gently. Makes 6 servings.

Lucille Moody   Nashville, Tennessee

FLOUNDER FILLET IN HERB SAUCE

4 ribs celery, chopped fine
2 tsps. onion, minced
3 T. butter or margarine
2 tsps. dill (or to taste)
½ tsp. tarragon
1 cup sour cream

2½ cups condensed mushroom
  soup
1 tsp. parsley
2 tsps. Dijon mustard
  salt and pepper to taste
16 oz. frozen fillet flounder,
  thawed

Preheat oven to 375°. Sauté celery and onion in butter until tender. Add remaining ingredients, except fish, and mix well. Pour into a shallow 10x16 inch casserole. Lay the fish fillets in the sauce, spooning some over fish. Bake for 20-25 minutes. Serves 6.

Pat Pringle   Phoenix, Arizona

RED SNAPPER AND CREOLE SAUCE

4 lbs. red snapper
1 pt. oyster, drained
2 lbs. peeled, raw shrimp
1 (4 oz.) can sliced mushrooms, drained

¼ cup sherry wine
1 lemon, thinly sliced
2 T. chopped parsley

Place fillets in large rectangular casserole dish. Sprinkle oyster, shrimp and mushrooms over fish. Cover with Creole Sauce. Sprinkle with wine, the lemon slices and parsley. Bake 20-25 minutes at 350°. Serve over rice. Serves 12-15.

CREOLE SAUCE

½ cup flour
¼ cup bacon drippings
2 cups chopped onion
1 cup chopped green onion
1 cup chopped green pepper
2 cloves garlic, minced
1 cup chopped celery and leaves
1 tsp. thyme
2 bay leaves

3 tsps. salt
½ tsp. pepper
1 (16 oz.) can tomatoes
1 (6 oz.) can tomato paste
1 (8 oz.) can tomato sauce
1 tsp. Tabasco
½ cup chopped parsley
1 T. lemon juice
½ cup sherry wine

In a large skillet or Dutch oven make a dark brown roux using the flour and bacon drippings. Add onions, green pepper, garlic, celery, thyme, bay leaves, salt and pepper. Saute over medium heat until onions are soft. Add tomatoes, tomato paste and sauce. Cover and simmer over low heat about 2 hours, stirring occasionally. Add remaining ingredients. Stir, cover and remove from heat. Let stand several hours before pouring over fish. Makes about 6 cups sauce.

Bea Campbell   Columbus, Georgia

SCALLOPED OYSTERS

1 ½ pts. large oysters
½ small lemon, juiced
6 T. butter, melted

1 cup crackers, crushed
½ cup milk

Drain oysters. Add lemon juice to melted butter. Butter shallow baking dish and put in a layer of oysters, half the crackers and half the lemon butter. Repeat to form a second layer. Add sufficient rich milk to moisten. Bake 30 minutes at 350°.

Donna Barker   Garden Grove, California

EASY BAKED FISH

1 lb. fish fillets, and type
salt to taste
white pepper to taste

onion powder to taste
¼ cup mayonnaise
paprika

Preheat oven to 325°. Line 8x10 inch dish with foil. Place fish in pan, sprinkle with seasonings. Use a pastry brush to sparingly coat tops and sides of fillets with mayonnaise. Top with generous sprinkling of paprika. Bake uncovered for about 20 minutes, until fish flakes when touched with a fork.

Note: No need to turn while baking. Any amount may be prepared by adjusting size of pan.

Carole Britton   Wilmington, Delaware

FISH FILLETS THERMIDOR

1 lb. fresh or thawed fish fillets
1 ½ cups milk
1 tsp. salt
¼ tsp. pepper

3 T. margarine, melted
3 T. flour
¼ lb. Cheddar cheese, grated
3 T. lemon juice

Preheat oven to 350°. Split fillets lengthwise and roll up. Fastening with a toothpick if necessary. Place in shallow 10x16 inch baking dish. Pour milk over fish. Add salt and pepper; bake 30 minutes. When done, pour off milk and add slowly to melted margarine into which the flour has been added. Add cheese and stir until melted. Add lemon juice and pour sauce over fillets. Brown quickly under broiler. Serves about 3-4.

Gerry Wright   San Jose, California

FISH IN WHITE WINE

3 lbs. fish
¾ cup white wine
½ cup water
1 onion, chopped
1 sprig parsley, chopped

1 sprig chervil, chopped
1 sprig thyme, chopped
2 bay leaves
salt and pepper
4 oz. margarine, in pats

Preheat oven to 350°. Place fish in a 9x13 baking dish. Mix wine with water and pour over fish. Place onion, parsley and chervil under and over fish. Add bay leaves and thyme. Top with salt, pepper and margarine. Bake 25-30 minutes. Dried herbs may be substituted for fresh if needed.

Becky Barns   Huntsville, Alabama

FRESH SHRIMP DISH

4 lettuce leaves
24 cooked, peeled shrimp
1 cup cottage cheese
4 slices lemon

Arrange lettuce leaves on 4 individual salad plates. Top with a scoop (¼ cup) of cottage cheese; surround with shrimp. Garnish with a lemon twist. Serve with Avocado Dressing.

Avocado Dressing
1 large avocado, peeled and pitted
1 cup sour cream
1 tsp. grated lemon peel
1 T. fresh lemon juice
2 tsps. prepared horseradish
½ tsp. salt

In a small bowl, mash avocado. Stir in remaining ingredients, mixing well. Cover with plastic wrap placed directly on top of dressing. Refrigerate 30 minutes. Serve 4.

Betty Bauer   Mission Viejo, California

79

SOLE PROVENCAL

1 lb. sole fillets
1 cup onion, chopped
½ cup celery, diced
¼ cup Planters oil
1 can (1 lb. size) tomatoes

2 T. parsley, chopped
2 bay leaves
1 ¼ tsps. salt
¼ tsp. pepper

In a large skillet saute the onion celery in the Planters Oil, until tender. Add the tomatoes, parsley, bay leaves, salt and pepper. Cover and simmer gently for 20 minutes. Add sole fillets, and continue cooking 10 minutes, or until fish flakes easily with a fork. Remove fish to warm platter. If a thicker sauce is desired, add a small amount of flour and cook until mixture is thickened and starts to boil. Makes 4 servings.

Heather White   Little Rock, Arkansas

SALMON SOUFFLE

WHITE SAUCE
2 T. butter
¼ tsp. pepper
1 ½ cups milk

3 T. flour
¼ tsp. salt

ADD TO SAUCE
2 cups flaked salmon
3 egg yolks (save whites)

1 T. onion, chopped

Mix egg yolks in white sauce and add onion and salmon. Beat egg whites until stiff and fold in just before placing in oven. Bake at 375° F. in medium buttered dish for 30 minutes or until center is firm.

Pete Lansbery   Robinson, Illinois

KEDGEREE OF CRAB

2 T. butter
2 T. flour
½ cup milk
1 cup sour cream

1 to 2 lbs. cooked King Crab
4 minced hard cooked eggs
2 T. white table wine
1 pkg. saffron rice, cooked

Melt butter in saucepan. Stir in flour gradually and bubble for one minute. Remove from heat and very slowly stir in milk. Return to heat and continue stirring until sauce thickens. Mix in sour cream. Add cooked crab, cooled eggs, and wine. Salt and pepper to taste. Simmer gently until heated. Serve over warm bed of Saffron rice. Serves 4.

Mrs. Robert Cable   Glendale, California

CRAB NEWBURG

1 lb. fresh lump crabmeat	2 T. onion, chopped
½ lb. butter	2 cups cream
3 T. flour	3 egg yolks lightly beaten, with
½ tsp. salt	2 T. sherry
1 tsp. paprika	6 slices toast, buttered

Melt butter in saucepan. Stir in flour, seasonings and chopped onion. Gradually stir in cream. Cook, stirring constantly until thickened and smooth. Add crabmeat and heat to serving temperature. Remove from heat. Stir in egg yolks. Serve on buttered toast. Serves 6.

Beth Toller   Montgomery, Alabama

BROILED LOBSTER TAILS

6 small frozen lobster tails	Salt and pepper to taste
Melted butter	

Thaw lobster. With a kitchen scissors, cut along the inner edges of the soft undershell, clipping off fins along the outer edges. Peel back and discard the soft undershell. Bend back the overshell to crack some of the joints and prevent curling. Place lobster tail, meat side up, on a greased broiler rack 2 inches from heat. Brush meat with melted butter; sprinkle with salt and pepper. Broil 15 to 20 minutes or until browned. Turn; broil 5 to 10 minutes. Serve with melted butter.

Jean Haughton   Fort Lauderdale, Florida

BOULLABAISSE
Serves approximately 8

1 small lobster tail	8 ozs. salted fish
8 ozs. filet of sole	16 ozs. red snapper
8 ozs. scallops	16 ozs. cod fish
1 ½ cup celery	1 to 1 ½ cups celery
1 to 1 ½ cups onions	½ cup parsley

Note: Dice all ingredients

1 lb. butter	2 bay leaves
sprinkle of thyme	3 qts. water

Saute all vegetables in butter. Add seafood, vegetables and spices to water and cook. Add ½ cup Chablis and ½ cup cornstarch, diluted in ½ cup water; cook additional ½ hour.

Chef Gus Pavlakis   Florissant, Missouri

POACHED FISH IN GALLIANO BUTTER

⅔ **cup slivered blanched almonds**
⅔ **cup butter**
¼ **cup Galliano liqueur**
¼ **cup lemon juice**
1 **T. dried dill**
   salt and pepper
2 **lbs. fillet of sole**

In a large skillet, saute almonds in butter until lightly toasted, browning butter. Add Galliano, lemon juice and seasonings; add sole. Cover and cook over medium heat 7 to 10 minutes until fish flakes easily with a fork. Spoon Galliano butter over fish often as it cooks. Serves 6.

Susan Gibbs   El Paso, Texas

MARINARA SAUCE FOR FISH

2 T. vegetable oil
1 clove garlic, minced
2 T. chopped parsley
1 16 oz. can tomatoes
1 8-oz. can tomato sauce

1 tsp. salt
Dash of pepper
½ tsp. sugar
¼ tsp. oregano

Combine all ingredients in a saucepan and simmer 10 minutes. Serve hot over fish. Makes about 1 ½ pints.

Tammy Jackson   Miami, Florida

CELERY SAUCE

2 T. butter
2 T. flour
2 cups milk

salt
pepper
1 cup finely chopped celery

Melt butter; stir in flour, blending well. Slowly add milk, stirring constantly. Simmer until thickened. Season to taste with salt and pepper. Add celery and heat. Serve hot over salmon loaf or fish patties. Makes 2 cups sauce.

Fara Bent   Sarasota, Florida

GALA SEAFOOD COCKTAIL SAUCE

¾ cup chili sauce
2 to 4 T. lemon juice
1 T. prepared horseradish

2 tsps. Worcestershire sauce
½ tsp. grated onion

Combine all ingredients, mixing well; chill; serve as a sauce for clams, shrimp or oysters. Makes 1 ¼ cups sauce.

Lorene Edwards   Chicago, Illinois

DILL SAUCE

1 cup sour cream
½ cup freshly chopped dill and
stems or 1 tsp. chopped dill
weed

½ cup freshly chopped parsley

In blender, combine sour cream with chopped fresh dill and mix on high speed for 20 seconds. Heat over hot water until luke-warm; do not boil. Chill; sauce will set in a few minutes. Serve cold. Makes 1 cup sauce.

Barbara Hanes   Peoria, Illinois

Fish and Seafood Notes

Ask the person whose card appears on the inside front cover of this book for a recipe form to submit your family favorite fish and seafood for next year's national cookbook.

Casseroles and Egg Dishes

TURKEY OR CHICKEN CASSEROLE

1 to 2 cups left over chicken or
turkey
2 cans Cream of Mushroom soup
2 cans of water (soup cans)
1 can milk (soup can)

½ cup dry white wine or
dry Sherry
2 envelopes Onion soup
mix
2-2½ cups rice (not Minute
Rice)

Mix all ingredients together. Bake about 1 ½ hours or until rice is done in 350° oven.

Judy McElhaney   Fort Washington, Maryland

BREAKFAST BRUNCH

12 slices bread
 6 slices Canadian bacon, cooked
(ham, Spam, chicken or bacon
may be substituted)

1 pkg. (12 oz.) shredded
cheddar cheese
6 eggs
4½ cups milk

Remove crusts from bread and butter one side. Place 6 slices, butter side down, on buttered 9x13 inch pan. Cover with your choice of meat, add the cheese, then place the other 6 slices of bread, butter side up over cheese. Beat eggs with milk and pour over bread. Refrigerate 12 hours. Bake 45 minutes to 1 hour at 350°. Makes 10-12 servings.

Deanna Penning   Bethesda, Maryland

EGG SAUSAGE CASSEROLE

1 lb. sausage
6 eggs
6 slices bread, cubed
2 cups milk

2 tsp. dry mustard
1 lb. grated sharp cheddar
cheese (less may be used)
1 tsp. salt

Brown sausage and drain. Cool. Beat eggs and add milk, bread, mustard and salt. Add cheese and cooled sausage. Put into ungreased casserole and bake 30 to 45 minutes in a 350° oven or until golden on top and inserted knife comes out clean.

Darleen Kelly   Holland, Michigan

LASAGNA ROLL UPS

Lasagna noodles
Sliced boiled Ham
Swiss cheese slices

Large jar spaghetti sauce
Mozzarella cheese, grated

Cook amount of noodles desired. Each noodle makes one roll up. Drain noodles. When cool enough to handle, make roll ups as follows: Lay noodle flat. In the middle of each place a slice of ham folded in half and slice of swiss cheese folded. Fold each end of noodle over middle. Pour half of sauce in bottom of pan. Place noodle, with folded side down, in sauce until all noodles are used. Pour rest of sauce on top of noodles. Sprinkle grated mozzarella cheese on top. Cover pan with foil. Bake at 350° for 30 minutes.

Delores Woodside   Cahokia, Illinois

"FEED THE CROWD" CASSEROLE

2 lbs. ground chuck
1 can (12 oz.) whole corn
1 cup chopped onions
¼ cup chopped pimientos
3 cups noodles, cooked
1 cup soft bread crumbs, buttered

1 can cream of chicken soup
1 can cream of mushroom soup
1 carton (8 oz.) sour cream
¾ tsp. salt
¼ tsp. pepper

Brown the meat, then add the onions and cook at medium temperature for 10 more minutes. Add remaining ingredients except the buttered bread crumbs. Pour into a 2 ½ quart casserole (or if you plan to freeze some, one 1 ½ quart and one 1 quart casserole) and top with the bread crumbs. Bake at 350° for 30 minutes. Serves 8 to 10.

Georgie M. Booker   Atlanta, Georgia

HASH BROWN CASSEROLE

1 pkg. (2 lb.) frozen hash browns
2 cans cream of chicken soup
1 carton (16 oz.) sour cream
1 cup onion flakes

1 small pkg. shredded cheddar cheese
20 Ritz crackers, crushed
1 stick melted margarine

Combine soup, sour cream and onion flakes. Put hash browns in a 9x13 inch pan and spread with soup mixture. Sprinkle shredded cheese over soup. Sprinkle cracker crumbs over cheese then drizzle with melted margarine. Bake at 350° for 1 hour. Serves 12.

Betty Jacobs   Honolulu, Hawaii

POTATO OMELET

2 T. butter
2 medium-size potatoes, pared and thinly sliced
½ cup sliced onion
1 T. minced parsley
⅛ tsp. paprika
4 eggs
¼ cup milk
½ tsp. salt
Freshly ground black pepper
1 small tomato, chopped

Melt butter in 10-inch skillet. Add next 4 ingredients; cover; cook 5 minutes over low heat stirring twice. Uncover; cook 3 to 5 minutes until potatoes are golden brown and tender. Beat eggs, milk, salt and pepper in bowl. Pour over potatoes; cook until eggs are almost set, about 3 minutes. Slide onto serving plate; spoon tomato on top. Serve immediately.

Judy McElhaney   Ft. Washington, Maryland

CHICKEN CASSEROLE CHINESE STYLE

2 T. butter
½ cup chopped onion
3 cups chopped celery
1 cup mushrooms or 1 8 oz. can, drained
1 T. soy sauce
½ cup broken cashew nuts

2 cups cooked chicken
1 can Cream of Mushroom soup
1 can Cream of Celery soup
3 T. milk
1 4 oz. can chow mein noodles

Melt butter. Add onion and celery. Cook 10 minutes or until tender. Add rest of ingredients, except for the nuts and ½ cup chow mein noodles. Put in ungreased casserole. Sprinkle with nuts and ½ cup chow mein noodles. Bake uncovered at 350° for 25 minutes. You can also use turkey, veal or any left over meat.

Barbara Kraetsch   Wauwatosa, Wisconsin

BREAKFAST PUDDING

⅓ cup sugar
1 tsp. salt
3 T. butter or margarine

5 cups milk
1 cup enriched cornmeal
3 eggs, beaten

Combine sugar, salt, margarine and 4 cups of the milk. Heat to scalding. Combine cornmeal and the remaining 1 cup milk, slowly pour into hot milk mixture, stirring constantly. Cook until thickened, stirring frequently. Cook covered over low heat 5 minutes, stir frequently. Stir a small amount of hot cornmeal mixture into beaten eggs. Quickly add egg mixture into hot cornmeal mixture, stirring constantly. Cook covered over low heat 5 minutes. Spoon into serving bowls. Sprinkle with freshly grated nutmeg. Makes 6 servings.

Carlene Baumheuter   Cahokia, Illinois

BROCCOLI CASSEROLE

1 pkg. frozen chopped broccoli; thawed and well drained
½ cup chopped celery
½ cup chopped green pepper
1 small onion, minced

2 cups Minute Rice; cooked in 2 cups water
1 can cream of chicken soup
½ cup milk
1 oz. Velveeta cheese

Fry vegetables in butter until tender, than add remaining ingredients. Pour in casserole dish and bake for 30 minutes at 350°.

Margaret Glover   Rhinelander, Wisconsin

GEORGIE'S MEAT-NOODLE CASSEROLE

1 lb. ground meat	2 cans (8 oz.) tomato sauce
1 pkg. (8 oz.) noodles	with mushrooms
½ pint sour cream	½ tsp. Worcestershire sauce
1 pkg. (3 oz.) cream cheese	1 medium onion; minced (or
½ cup grated cheddar cheese	substitute 2 T. dry minced
	onion)

Brown the meat, then add the mixed combination of tomato sauce, onion and Worcestershire sauce. Cook together on low to medium heat for 20 minutes; allow to cool for 15 minutes. Cook the noodles as directed on package, cool for 15 minutes; then mix in the sour cream and cream cheese with the noodles. Layer pan or dish with an alternating layer of noodles and meat sauce (beginning and ending with the noodles). Bake at 350° for 30 to 45 minutes. Serves 6 to 8.

Georgie M. Booker   Atlanta, Georgia

PIZZA CASSEROLE

12 oz. wide noodles	2 tsp. salt
1½ lbs. ground beef	2 cups shredded mozzarella
3 cups pizza sauce	cheese

Cook noodles in salted water for 2-3 minutes; drain. Brown ground beef; drain off fat. Add sauce, salt and pepper to ground beef. Put half of noodles in a greased 9x13 inch pan, cover with half of the sauce and cheese. Repeat layers. Bake at 350° for 30 minutes. Serves 12.

Yvonne Pepper   Baton Rouge, Louisiana

GRIDIRON CASSEROLE

1 medium onion, chopped fine	½ tsp. pepper
1 tsp. salt	1 cup water
1 can tomato soup	1 medium can whole kernel
1 pkg. (6 oz.) noodles	corn or 1 small pkg. frozen
1 cup grated Velveeta cheese	corn
1 lb. hamburger	

Brown onion and hamburger, add salt, pepper, tomato soup and water. Cook noodles in boiling salted water until tender; drain and add to meat mixture with corn. Pour into a greased casserole and sprinkle grated cheese over top. Bake at 375° for 20 minutes. Makes 6 servings.

Mrs. Dorothy J. Vogel   Fulton, Illinois

CHICKEN BROCCOLI CASSEROLE

1 pkg. shredded cheddar cheese
1 pkg. frozen broccoli, cooked
4 cups cooked chicken, cubed

1 can cream of chicken soup
½ cup Minute Rice, cooked

Grease casserole dish and layer ingredients in the following order: chicken, broccoli, rice, cheese and soup. Repeat layers in the same order except the top layer should end with cheese. Bake at 350° for 30 minutes. Makes 6 servings.

Robin McCasland   Atlanta, Georgia

SPINACH FANDANGO

1 lb. ground beef
2 10 oz. pkgs. frozen spinach
1 medium onion, chopped
1 can cream of celery soup
1 clove of garlic
1 8 oz. sour cream
1 8 oz. can chopped
  mushrooms

1 tsp. oregano
¼ cup cooking oil
2 large slices mozzarella
  cheese
  salt and pepper to taste
  lasagna noodles

Brown meat, onions, garlic, mushrooms and oregano in oil, season with salt and pepper. Place frozen spinach on top of beef mixture, cover and let steam thaw spinach until able to mix together. Mix in soup and sour cream; pour into casserole dish layered with the noodles. Top with cheese slices and bake at 350° F. for 15 to 20 minutes. Serves 8.

Debbie Petrus   Ballwin, Missouri

SIX CAN CASSEROLE
Serves 5 to 6

3 or 4 chicken breasts, cooked
  and cubed
1 can mushrooms, drained
1 can chow mein noodles
1 small onion, chopped
  salt and pepper to taste

1 can cream of chicken soup
1 can water chestnuts,
  drained and sliced
¾ to 1 can evaporated milk
1 cup celery, cut up
  paprika, to taste

Combine in casserole and bake at 350° F. for about 45 minutes.

Katie Barrett   Cary, Illinois

JACK-POT CASSEROLE

1 lb. round steak, ground	4 oz. noodles
2 T. fat	2½ cups cream style corn
¼ cup chopped onion	¼ cup chopped ripe olives
1 can tomato soup	1 cup grated American
1½ cups water	cheese

Brown meat in hot fat. Add onion. Cook until golden brown. Add tomato soup, water and noodles. Cook until noodles are tender, stirring frequently. Season to taste. Add corn, olives and cheese. Pour into greased 2 quart casserole and sprinkle with a little more grated cheese. Bake at 350° for 45 minutes. Serves 8.

Alice Owens   Cincinnati, Ohio

BRUNCH EGG CASSEROLE

2 cups plain croutons	½ tsp. mustard
4 oz. Cheddar cheese, grated	⅛ tsp. onion powder
4 eggs, beaten	dash of pepper
2 cups milk	4 slices bacon, crumbles
½ tsp. salt	

Put croutons and cheese in bottom of a greased 10x6x1¾ inch casserole dish. Combine eggs, milk, salt, pepper, mustard and onion powder; mix until blended. Pour over croutons and sprinkle with crumbled bacon. Bake 1 hour or until eggs are set at 325°. Serves 6.

Vera Halbert   Austin, Texas

BAKED OMELET

¼ cup margarine	Dash of pepper
1½ doz. eggs	1 cup grated cheese
1 cup sour cream	Mushrooms, 1 cup; cooked
1 cup milk	bacon, 1 cup; diced ham
1 tsp. salt	(optional)
¼ cup chopped onions	

Place margarine in pan and melt in 325°F. oven. Mix all remaining ingredients with mixer. Pour into pan (make sure margarine covers bottom of pan). Bake about 35 minutes, or until firm and golden brown.

Clara Duvall   Arlington, Virginia

LASAGNA CASSEROLE

¼ cup vegetable oil
2 cloves garlic, minced
1 medium onion, chopped
2 ribs celery, sliced
1 29-oz. can tomato sauce
1 6-oz. can tomato paste
1 6-oz. can water
1 tsp. salt
¼ tsp. pepper
¼ tsp. oregano
¼ tsp. nutmeg
½ lb. Italian sausage
1 lb. lasagna
1 lb. ricotta cheese
1 cup grated mozzarella cheese
½ cup grated Romano cheese

Heat oil in a large saucepan. Add garlic, and onions and sauté for three to five minutes, or until onions are transparent. Add celery, tomato sauce, tomato paste, water, salt, pepper, oregano and nutmeg. Reduce heat and cook for one hour. Prick sausage with fork and place in a baking dish. Bake at 375° for 25 minutes. Prepare lasagna according to package directions and drain. In a greased six-quart casserole, layer lasagna, tomato mixture, ricotta cheese, mozzarella cheese and sausage, ending with sauce and cheese. Sprinkle Romano cheese on top. Bake at 375° for 30 minutes, or until cheese is golden. Serves 4 to 6.

Sandra Lawson   Martinez, Georgia

*F*amily *F*avorite Casserole and Egg Dish Notes

Ask the person whose card appears on the inside front cover of this book for a recipe form to submit your family favorite casseroles and egg dishes for next year's national cookbook.

Desserts, Pies and Cakes

LEMON LUSH DESSERT

Crust:

1 cup flour   ½ cup chopped nuts
½ cup margarine

Mix together flour, margarine and nuts and press into a 9x13 pan. Bake in 325° oven for 25 minutes, then cool to room temperature.

Filling:

1 cup Cool Whip (out of an 8 oz.   1 pkg. (8 oz.) cream cheese
  container)
1 cup powdered sugar

Combine Cool Whip, powdered sugar and cream cheese and spread evenly over the cooled crust.

2 small pkgs. lemon instant   3 cups milk
  pudding mix

Combine pudding mix and milk and pour over the first layer.

Topping:

Spread the remainder of the container of Cool Whip over the top. Chill before serving. Makes approximately 12 servings.

Jessimine M. Wilkens   El Paso, Texas

NUTTY TEACAKES

2 cups sugar   dash salt
2 sticks margarine   1 cup chopped pecans
1 tsp. vanilla   2 tsps. baking powder
3 eggs   1 tsp. soda
½ cup buttermilk   3½ to 4 cups flour

Cut sugar into margarine. Mix buttermilk and eggs; add to sugar, add vanilla, salt, soda, baking powder, then add pecans. Add 3½ to 4 cups flour, depending on humidity. Bake on buttered aluminum cookie sheet for 15 minutes or until light brown. Cool on cookie rack. Makes 80 cookies.

Bill Johnson   Dallas, Texas

FRESH FRUIT PARFAIT

1 orange peeled and cut in bite-size pieces
1 banana cut into pieces
1 apple cut into pieces

Dressing
½ cup sour cream
½ cup marshmallow creme
1 T. orange peel
2 T. orange juice

In a small bowl, combine sour cream, marshmallow creme, orange peel and orange juice. Stir until smooth. Layer fruit and dressing in 4 parfait glasses.

Joan Smith   Cleveland, Ohio

98

HI-HO DELIGHT

60 Hi-Ho crackers, crushed finely
4 T. sugar
1 stick butter, melted
1 can Eagle Brand milk
1 can (small) frozen orange juice, undiluted

2 (11 oz.) cans Mandarin oranges, drained, cut into pieces
1 (20 oz.) can crushed pineapple, drained
1 (12 oz.) carton Cool Whip

Mix together crackers, sugar and butter. Press into 9x13 pan. Save 1 cup of crumbs to put on top. In large bowl mix together Eagle Brand milk and orange juice. Add oranges, pineapple and fold in Cool Whip. Spread mixture over the cracker crumb crust. Sprinkle reserve cup of crumbs over top. Dot with Maraschino cherries, drained well. Chill in refrigerator.

Thelma Ancell   Joplin, Missouri

CHERRY DESSERT

2 cans cherry pie filling
1 pkg. dry white cake mix
2 sticks margarine

½ cup coconut
½ cup chopped nuts

Grease a 9x13 inch pan. Spread pie filling on bottom, sprinkle the cake mix evenly on top. Melt margarine and spoon over this. Sprinkle on coconut and nuts. Bake at 350° for 40 minutes.

Polly Vineyard   Papillion, Nebraska

DATE TORTE

1¼ cups boiling water
1 tsp. baking soda
1 large box chopped dates
¾ cup shortening
1 cup sugar
2 eggs
1½ cups flour

½ tsp. salt
1 tsp. cinnamon
1 tsp. vanilla
½ cup chocolate chips
½ cup chopped walnuts
½ cup sugar

Combine boiling water, baking soda and dates, let cool. Cream together shortening, sugar and eggs. Add flour, salt, cinnamon and the cooled dates. Mix well and add the vanilla. Pour into a greased and floured 9x13 inch pan. Sprinkle the chocolate chips, walnuts and sugar over top. Bake at 350° for 40-45 minutes. Serves 15.

Patricia Gleason   New Paltz, New York

BLITZ TORTE

1 ⅓ cups flour
1 tsp. baking powder
⅛ tsp. salt
½ cup shortening or oleo

1 ¼ cups sugar
4 eggs; separated
1 tsp. vanilla
4 T. milk

TOPPING:
½ cup sliced almonds
1 T. sugar

½ tsp. cinnamon
4 pkgs. (¾ oz.) vanilla pudding

Sift flour, baking powder and salt together. Cream shortening with ½ cup sugar until fluffy. Add well beaten egg yolks, vanilla, milk and sifted dry ingredients. Spread mixture in two greased 9 inch round pans. Beat egg whites until stiff but not dry. Add remaining sugar gradually and beat until egg whites hold sharp peak. Spread meringue over unbaked mixture in both pans. Sprinkle with almonds and sugar-cinnamon mixture. Bake at 350° for 30 minutes. Cool and remove from pans. Fill with pudding mix (cooked and cooled).

Gertrude Gajardo   Lexington, Kentucky

FIVE DAY COCONUT CAKE

2 cups fresh grated coconut
2 cups sugar
2 cups sour cream

1 Duncan Hines yellow cake
mix
1 can Angel Flake coconut

Five days before planning to serve—Mix fresh coconut, sugar and sour cream. Refrigerate, uncovered 24 hours. Bake cake according to instructions in 2 layers. Cool. Cut each layer crosswise to make 4 layers in all. Spread sour cream mixture between layers and on top. Top with Angel Flake coconut. Refrigerate, covered, for 4 days before serving. Serves 18 to 20.

Mrs. Elmer Z. Delp   New Holland, Pennsylvania

PEACH CRISP

1 (29 oz.) can sliced peaches,
undrained
1 pkg. Betty Crocker Butter
Pecan cake mix

1 ½ sticks margarine, melted
1 cup coconut
1 cup chopped pecans

Starting with peaches, layer above in ungreased 9x13 pan. Bake at 325° for 55 to 60 minutes.

Nancy Lorenz   Ithaca, New York

101

PUMPKIN TORTE

24 graham crackers, crushed   ½ cup butter, melted
⅓ cup sugar

Mix together and press in a 9x13 inch pan.

2 eggs   1 pkg. (8 oz.) cream cheese,
¾ cup sugar   softened

Combine ingredients and pour over crust and bake for 20 minutes at 350°.

2 cups pumpkin   ½ tsp. salt
3 egg yolks   1 T. cinnamon
½ cup sugar   dash of ground cloves
½ cup milk

Cook all ingredients in a saucepan till thickened. Remove from heat.

1 envelope plain gelatin   ½ cup cold water

Dissolve gelatin in cold water and add to pumpkin mixture. Cool.

3 egg whites   ¼ cup sugar

Beat egg whites, combine with sugar and add to cooled pumpkin mixture. Pour pumpkin mixture over cooled crust and top with whipped cream. Refrigerate several hours before serving. Makes 15 generous servings.

Tina McMullen   Cherry Hill, New Jersey

APPLE PIE

Crust:
2 cups flour   dash of salt
1 cup Crisco   ½ cup cold water

Blend flour, Crisco and salt together. Add water and mix well.

Filling:
butter   2 tsps. apple pie spice
1 cup sugar   apples
1 tsp. flour

Slice apples into crust and sprinkle with mixture of sugar, flour and pie spice. Dab butter over pie and cover with top crust. Poke holes in top crust and bake 1 hour at 400°.

Carole Nielsen   Omaha, Nebraska

COCONUT DELIGHT

½ cup margarine; room
  temperature
½ cup powdered sugar
3 eggs, separated; room
  temperature
  juice of 1 lemon or 3 T.
  ReaLemon

1 angel food cake (loaf cake
  works best)
1 container (8 oz.) Cool Whip
  flaked coconut for topping

Cream together margarine and sugar. Add egg yolks one at a time, beat well. Fold stiffly beaten egg whites into egg yolk mixture. Add lemon juice and ½ container of Cool Whip. Line a 13x9 inch pan with slices of angel food cake. Pour ½ of mixture over cake. Add another layer of cake and remaining egg mixture. Top with remaining Cool Whip and sprinkle generously with coconut. Refrigerate overnight. Makes 10 servings. IMPORTANT: It is absolutely essential that the margarine and eggs are ROOM TEMPERATURE, otherwise the egg mixture will not blend together properly.

Carol Statham

Las Vegas, Nevada

MYSTERY PUDDING

1 #2 can fruit cocktail
1 egg, beaten
1 cup sugar
1½ cups flour

1 tsp. soda
½ tsp. salt
2 T. shortening

Mix the above and put into a greased casserole. Top with ½ cup brown sugar mixed with ½ cup chopped nuts. Bake at 350° for 30 to 35 minutes. May be served with whipped or ice cream.

Bessie Blakely

Zenith, Washington

BAKED BANANAS WITH RUM AND BUTTER

4 T. (½ stick) unsalted butter
4 Medium bananas, peeled and
  halved lengthwise

¼ cup brown sugar
¼ cup dark rum

Preheat oven to 400°. Butter glass baking dish large enough to hold all bananas in one layer. Put bananas, cut side down, in dish. Sprinkle with sugar and rum, and dot with remaining butter. Bake until sugar is melted and bananas are tender but not mushy, about 10 minutes. Serve hot.

Cheri Emery

Arlington, Texas

CHOCOLATE PIE

1 Baked pie crust
   or graham crackers crust
1 large instant chocolate pudding
1 cup cold milk
2 cups (1 pt.) softened vanilla ice cream
1 6 oz. Cool Whip
   Almonds or sweet chocolate

Mix pudding and milk together add softened ice cream and mix well. Fill pie shell and refrigerate until set. Generously frost pie with Cool Whip. Top with almonds or shaved sweet chocolate.

Mary Johnson   Bethel Park, Pennsylvania

104

APRICOT DREAM

3 cups vanilla wafer crumbs
2 (large) cans apricots
1 cup chopped pecans

½ pint whipping cream, whipped

Sauce:
½ cup butter, melted
1 cup sugar

2 eggs, beaten

Combine the sauce ingredients and cook over low flame, stirring constantly, until thickened. Set aside until cooled. Spread ½ of the wafer crumbs over the bottom of a 15x10 pan. Spread the cooled sauce over the crumbs and follow with ½ the whipped cream. Arrange the apricots over the cream and sprinkle with chopped pecans. Top with the remaining whipped cream and sprinkle the rest of the wafer crumbs over the top. Chill for 24 hours.

Harriet Phelps   Charlotte, North Carolina

SOUR CREAM CHEESE CAKE

Crust:
1 ¼ cups graham cracker crumbs
¼ cup sugar

¼ cup melted butter or margarine

Filling:
2 pkgs. (8 oz.) cream cheese
½ cup sugar

3 eggs
¾ tsp. vanilla

Topping:
1 pint sour cream
½ cup sugar

1 tsp. vanilla

Crust:
Mix together graham cracker crumbs, sugar and melted butter. Press into a spring form pan and chill a short time.

Filling:
Using a mixer beat cream cheese, sugar, eggs and vanilla until smooth. Pour into crust-lined pan and bake at 375° for 20 minutes. Remove from oven and cool for 15 minutes.

Topping:
Mix sour cream, sugar and vanilla. Pour over top of cake. Increase oven to 475° and bake for 10 minutes.

Eleanor Nartker   Chicago, Illinois

CHERRY CONCOCTION

2 (16 oz.) cans red tart cherries	¾ cup pecans, chopped
1¼ cups small marshmallows	3 large or 4 small bananas

Drain cherries, reserving ½ cup juice. Dice bananas, add pecans, marshmallows and cherries. Well cooled cream dressing is stirred into fruit and nuts along with ½ cup cherry juice. Refrigerate.

Cream dressing:

1 cup sweet cream	3 T. flour
1 cup sugar	

Blend sugar and flour in saucepan; add cream and cook until thickened, stirring constantly. Allow to cool.

Jan Ryan

Burington, North Carolina

JACK DANIELS CAKE

1 box Yellow cake mix	1½ sticks margarine
1 box instant Vanilla pudding	1 (16 oz.) pkg. butterscotch
5 eggs, slightly beaten	chips
½ cup milk	1 cup black walnuts
½ cup Jack Daniels	

Sift cake mix and instant pudding together. Add eggs, milk, Jack Daniels and margarine and beat long and hard. Add butterscotch chips and black walnuts, retaining ¼ cup of each. Pour batter into a prepared 9x13 pan and sprinkle the remaining chips and nuts over the top of the batter. Bake at 350 degrees for 45 to 60 minutes.

Billie Wilkens

Oronogo, Missouri

PUMPKIN ICE CREAM PIE

1 10 inch graham cracker crumb pie shell	1 tsp. cinnamon
1 pint vanilla ice cream	¼ tsp. ginger
1 cup cooked pumpkin	¼ tsp. nutmeg
1 cup sugar	¼ tsp. salt
	1 cup whipped cream

Spread layer of ice cream in bottom of pie shell. In saucepan combine pumpkin, sugar, cinnamon, ginger, nutmeg and salt. Cook 3 minutes. Cool and fold in whipped cream. Spread mixture over ice cream layer. Freeze.

Janet Ostling

Louisville, Kentucky

MISSOURI SHEATHE CAKE

Cake:

2 cups sugar	4 T. cocoa
2 cups flour	1 cup water
1 tsp. baking soda	½ cup buttermilk
1 tsp. cinnamon	2 eggs, beaten
¼ lb. margarine	1 tsp. vanilla
½ cup shortening	

Frosting:

1 stick margarine	1 box powdered sugar
4 T. cocoa	1 tsp. vanilla
6 T. milk	1 cup nuts, chopped (walnuts or pecans)

Cake:
Sift together in a mixing bowl sugar, flour, baking soda and cinnamon. Bring to boil but DO NOT COOK margarine, shortening, cocoa and water. Pour over dry ingredients. Mix and add buttermilk, eggs and vanilla. Mix well and pour into greased cookie sheet 15 ½ x 10 ½ x 1. Bake at 400 degrees for 20 minutes.

Frosting:
Bring to a boil the margarine, cocoa and milk. Remove from heat and add the powdered sugar, vanilla and nuts. Pour over hot cake. Start icing 5 minutes before cake is done.

Elsie Richey   Lamar, Missouri

CHOCOLATE NUT ZUCCHINI CAKE

3 sq. unsweeted chocolate	4 eggs
3 cups unsifted all purpose flour	3 cups sugar
1 ½ tsp. baking powder	1 ¼ cups salad oil
1 tsp. baking soda	3 cups finely grated zucchini
1 tsp. salt	1 cup nuts

Preheat oven 350°. Grease well and flour a 10 inch tube pan. Melt chocolate over hot boiling water. Sift flour and baking powder, soda and salt, then set aside. In large bowl at high speed, beat eggs until thick and light. Gradually add sugar ¼ cup at a time, beating well after each addition, add salad oil, cooled chocolate, and beat until well blended. At low speed, add dry ingredients mixing until smooth. By wooden spoon blend in grated zucchini and nuts until well mixed. Bake 1 hour 15 minutes.

Tammy Bland   Michigan City, Indiana

FRESH COCONUT CAKE

1 pkg. White cake mix with
  pudding mix
⅔ cup buttermilk
⅓ cup water
3 eggs
1 tsp. vanilla
1 tsp. coconut flavor

1 cup Eagle Brand canned milk
1 (16 oz.) can Cream of
  Coconut
1 (9 oz.) container Cool Whip
2 pkgs. frozen fresh grated
  coconut

Mix cake according to directions on box except use the ⅔ cup buttermilk and ⅓ cup water. Bake in 350 degree oven in Pam sprayed 9x13 pan for 27 to 30 minutes. Combine Eagle Brand milk and Cream of Coconut. Punch holes in cake while hot. Pour the milk and coconut mixture over the cake. Cool. Spread with Cool Whip and sprinkle shredded coconut over top. Refrigerate.

Gene Metz

Lincoln, Nebraska

BLUEBERRY BUNDT CAKE

2½ cups all-purpose flour
1 cup sugar
½ tsp. salt
1 tsp. baking powder
1 tsp. baking soda
2 eggs, beaten
¾ cup cooking oil

1 cup sour cream
1 (8 oz.) pkg. dates, chopped
2 T. grated orange peel
½ cup almonds, chopped
1½ cups fresh blueberries or
  cranberries

Glaze:
1 cup powdered sugar, sighted
1 T. light corn syrup
2 tsps. imitation vanilla flavoring

2 tsps. imitation butter
  flavoring
2 tsps. imitation nut flavoring
2 tsps. milk

Preheat oven to 350 degrees. Grease bundt pan well. Dust with flour. In large bowl sift flour, salt, baking powder and baking soda. Add sugar and mix well. In separate bowl combine eggs, oil and sour cream; mix well. With wooden spoon mix liquid mixture into bowl with flour mixture well. Add dates, orange peel and nuts. Mix well. Carefully mix fruit into cake mixture so as not to crush berries. Pour batter into prepared pan. Bake for 1 hour. Cool 10 minutes in pan, then invert into serving plate.

Glaze:
Mix all ingredients together. Add ¼ tsp. milk if too thick. Dribble over warm cake.

Benny DeRosa

Ft. Lauderdale, Florida

TURTLE CAKE

1 box German Chocolate cake mix
14 oz. pkg. Kraft Caramels
½ cup or 1 small can evaporated milk
¾ cup butter
1 cup pecans
1 cup chocolate chips

Preheat oven to 350°. Prepare cake mix according to package directions. Pour ½ of the batter into a Pam sprayed 9x13 inch pan. Bake for only 15 minutes. In top of double boiler over hot water melt together the caramels, milk and butter. Pour this over baked portion of the cake. Sprinkle the pecans and chocolate chips over the caramel mixture. Spread remaining batter over caramel mixture. Bake an additional 25 to 30 minutes. If desired, you may before returning the cake to the oven, sprinkle ½ cup of the pecans over the top of the batter.

Thelma Ancell   Joplin, Missouri

Family Favorite

Dessert Notes

Ask the person whose card appears on the inside front cover of this book for a recipe form to submit your family favorite desserts, pies and cakes for next year's national cookbook.

Bars, Cookies and Candy

GERMAN CHOCOLATE BARS
makes 100 bars

14 oz. pkg. of Kraft Caramels*
1 pkg. German chocolate cake mix
¾ cup melted margarine or butter

12 oz. pkg. chocolate chips
⅓ cup evaporated milk*
⅓ cup evaporated milk
½ cup chopped walnuts

Melt caramels with ⅓ cup evaporated milk in a double boiler. Mix cake mix, ⅓ cup evaporated milk, butter or margarine and nuts. Place ⅔ of cake mix mixture in a 9x13 greased pan; bake at 350° F. for 3 minutes. Remove from oven and sprinkle chocolate chips on crust; pour hot caramel over chips. Top with remaining cake mixture, crumbled; return to oven for 15 to 18 minutes at 350° F. Cut into small bite-size bars.

Note: *Pat mixture flat to cover the bottom of pan. It forms a crust.

Eleanor Serrahn   Sturgeon Bay, Wisconsin

OATMEAL CARMELITAS
makes 18, 2 inch squares

1 ¼ cups flour
¾ cup brown sugar (packed)
¼ tsp. salt
1 cup semi-sweet chocolate pieces
¾ cup caramel flavored ice cream topping

1 cup rolled oats
½ tsp. baking soda
¾ cup butter or margarine (melted)
½ cup walnuts

Heat oven to 350° F.; combine 1 cup flour, oats, sugar, baking soda, salt and butter. Pat ¾ of mixture into a greased 9x9 pan; bake for 10 minutes. Remove from oven; sprinkle with chocolate pieces and walnuts. Combine caramel topping and ¼ cup flour and mix well; drizzle over top. Sprinkle remaining crumb mixture over caramel topping. Return to oven; bake 15 to 20 minutes until crumbs are golden brown.

Note: Chill before eating.

Mrs. Ceil Beaupre   Oneida, Wisconsin

PEANUT BUTTER BARS

½ cup butter
⅓ cup peanut butter
½ cup sugar
¼ cup brown sugar
1 egg
2 T. milk
1 tsp. vanilla
2¼ cups flour
¼ tsp. baking powder
¼ tsp. salt
2 1-oz. squares unsweetened chocolate, melted
  Salted peanuts, chopped
  Semisweet chocolate chips

Cream butter and peanut butter. Gradually add sugars, beating until light and fluffy. Add egg, milk and vanilla; beat well. Combine flour, baking powder and salt; gradually blend into creamed mixture. Divide dough into two parts, one slightly larger than the other. Add cooled chocolate to the smaller portion. Mix until evenly blended.

PEANUT BUTTER BARS

Divide chocolate dough in half; repeat for peanut butter dough. Roll out each dough between 2 sheets of waxed paper to form an 8-inch square. Invert one square of peanut butter dough on top of one square of chocolate dough, removing waxed paper. Invert remaining chocolate dough on top, then remaining peanut butter dough, to form four layers. Cover and chill several hours or overnight. Cut into thirty-two 2-inch bars. Place on cookie sheets. Bake in 350° oven 12 to 14 minutes. Drizzle with melted chocolate chips if desired. Makes 32 bars.

Bobbie Burkley   New Orleans, Louisiana

NO BAKE CHOCOLATE COOKIES

2 cups sugar
1 stick margarine
½ cup cocoa
1 tsp. vanilla

½ cup milk
½ cup peanut butter
3 cups quick cooking oatmeal

Combine sugar, margarine, cocoa, vanilla and milk; heat and bring to a boil for 1 minute. Remove from heat and add peanut butter and oatmeal. Mix well and drop teaspoonful on wax paper and chill.

Mrs. Larry Mays   Jefferson City, Missouri

FANTASY FUDGE
makes 3 lbs.

3 cups sugar
⅔ cup (5⅓ oz. can) evaporated
  milk
1 7 oz. jar marshmallow creme
1 12 oz. pkg. semi-sweet
  chocolate pieces

¾ cup margarine
1 cup chopped nuts
1 tsp. vanilla

Combine sugar, margarine and milk in heavy 2 ½ qt. saucepan; bring to a full boil, stirring constantly. Continue boiling for 5 minutes over medium heat, stirring constantly to prevent scorching; remove from heat. Stir in chocolate pieces until melted; add marshmallow creme, nuts, and vanilla. Beat until well blended; pour into greased 13x9 pan. Cool at room temperature; cut into squares.

Carol Higgins   Sturgeon Bay, Wisconsin

PEANUT BUTTER BALLS

1 cup margarine
½ cup crunchy peanut butter
½ cup chopped peanuts
1 cup flaked coconut
2¼ cups crushed graham
  crackers

1 tsp. vanilla
1 1 lb. box powdered sugar
1 12 oz. pkg. semisweet
  chocolate chips
⅔ cup grated paraffin

Melt margarine. Add other ingredients except chocolate and paraffin. Form into small balls and chill. Melt chocolate and paraffin in double boiler over hot water. Using 2 forks, dip balls into chocolate. Place on wax paper to dry. Yields 100 balls.

Peggy Stephens   Montgomery, Alabama

CHOCOLATE DROP COOKIES
makes 2 to 3 dozen

1 ½ cups sifted flour
1 tsp. baking powder
½ cup melted shortening
1 egg
1 tsp. vanilla

¼ tsp. salt
2 ozs. (or squares) of chocolate
1 cup brown sugar
½ cup milk

Sift flour, salt and baking powder together. Melt chocolate; add to melted shortening. Add sugar, egg, milk and vanilla. Blend thoroughly. Add sifted ingredients. Let stand 10 minutes. Drop from tsp. onto greased baking sheets. Bake in a 375° F. oven for 12 to 15 minutes. Frost, if you desire.

Judy Pender   Alexandria, Virginia

IGLOOS

1 box Butter cookies
1 cup sugar
1 (No. 2) can crushed pineapple
1 stick softened butter or margarine
1 cup raisins, chopped

1 cup nuts, chopped
1 pt. whipping cream
1 T. sugar
½ T. vanilla
coconut
maraschino cherries

Mix together sugar, pineapple, butter, raisins and nuts. Layer butter cookies alternately with mixture, using 4 cookies for each igloo. Let set at room temperature overnight. Cover each igloo with whipped cream. Sprinkle with coconut and decorate with a maraschino cherry.

Whipping cream:
Whip together cream, sugar and vanilla.

Marjorie Massie   Dupo, Illinois

RUM BALLS

3 cups vanilla wafers, crushed
1 cup confectioners' sugar
1 ½ cups nuts, finely chopped
1 ½ T. cocoa

2 T. light corn syrup
½ cup rum
Confectioners' sugar

Combine all ingredients and mix thoroughly. Form into small balls and roll in confectioners' sugar. Wrap in wax paper. They freeze well. Also better to allow flavor to mellow a few days. Yields 50.

Wilma Swyer   Lexington, Kentucky

DIVINITY

FIRST PART

3 cups sugar   1 cup clear corn syrup
1 cup water, boil to 260° F.

SECOND PART

1 cup sugar   ½ cup water, cook to 238° F.

THIRD PART

whites of 2 to 3 eggs   ¾ lb. pecans
½ lb. candied cherries

Add second part to first part; beat into the stiffly beaten egg whites. Add nuts and candied fruit. Drop onto waxed paper or pour into buttered pan and cut into square pieces.

Note: Never fails.

Maura Hackathorn   Los Angeles, California

ALMOND MACAROONS

1 (8 oz.) can almond paste   3 egg whites
¾ cup sugar   ½ tsp. almond extract
Pinch of salt

Break up and mash almond paste to soften; add other ingredients alternately and beat well. Line a cookie sheet with brown paper or foil. Squeeze small amounts of dough through a pastry tube or drop from a teaspoon 2 inches apart onto cookie sheet. Smooth tops with pastry brush moistened with water. Bake at 350° for 15-20 minutes or until golden and puffed. May be stored in airtight tin indefinitely or in freezer. Makes 40-50.

Irene Cassidy   Denver, Colorado

CHEESECAKE PUFFS

16 oz. cream cheese   1 tsp. vanilla
¾ cup sugar   24 vanilla wafers
2 eggs   22 oz. canned cherry pie filling

Preheat oven to 375°. Place the cream cheese, sugar eggs and vanilla in a large bowl and beat with electric mixer until smooth. Line muffin tins with paper liners and put one vanilla wafer in the bottom of each liner. Fill ¾ full with cheese mixture. Bake for 10 minutes and cool. Cover with pie filling. Chill. Yields 24.

Anne Barker   Davenport, Iowa

OATMEAL KRISPIES

1 cup shortening	1 tsp. baking soda
1 cup brown sugar	1 tsp. salt
1 cup sugar	1 tsp. vanilla
2 eggs	3 cups regular rolled oats
1½ cups flour	1 cup nuts, chopped

Cream shortening and sugar; add eggs and blend. Sift flour, soda and salt together. Mix into creamed mixture and add vanilla. Blend in oats and nuts. Shape into small rolls and chill overnight. Slice thinly and bake on greased cookie sheet at 375° for 10 minutes. 8 dozen.

Rita Simpson   Omaha, Nebraska

CHOCOLATE CHIP MERINGUES

2 egg whites (at room temperature)	¾ cup sugar
1 tsp. vanilla	1 cup chocolate chips
⅛ tsp. cream of tartar	½ cup chopped nuts

Beat first 3 ingredients until soft peaks form, add sugar one teaspoon at a time, beat until stiff peaks form. Fold in chocolate chips and nuts. Bake on cookie sheet covered with brown paper for 25 minutes at 300° F.

Jeanne Peterson   Arcadia, California

PUMPKIN BARS
makes about 20 bars

1 16 oz. can pumpkin	2 cups sugar
2 tsp. cinnamon	1 cup Crisco oil
4 eggs	1 cup nuts
2 cups flour	raisins (optional)

Mix all ingredients and pour into greased cookie sheet; bake at 325° F. for 25 minutes.

TOPPING

1 T. milk	1 tsp. vanilla
½ cup margarine	6 oz. cream cheese

Mix all ingredients together; add additional powder sugar for spreading consistency. Spread on bars while still hot.

Note: Substitute 3 T. coffee for powdered sugar, if desired.

Carol McDaniel   Washington, D.C.

WHITE FUDGE

1 ⅓ cups sugar
 ½ cup butter or margarine
 ⅔ cup non-dairy liquid coffee cream
 ⅛ tsp. salt
 ½ lb. white chocolate coating
 2 cups miniature marshmallows
 ½ tsp. vanilla
    nuts optional

Cook sugar, butter, non-dairy liquid coffee cream, salt, without stirring to 238°. Remove from heat and add white chocolate coating, marshmallows and vanilla. Blend well. Pack into a 9 inch square pan. When partially cool cut into squares.

Merle Healy   Lake Stevens, Washington

amily
avorite

Cookies and Candy
Notes

Ask the person whose card appears on the inside front cover of this book for a recipe form to submit your family favorite bars, cookies and candy for next year's national cookbook.

Pot Pourri

COUNTRY BAKED APPLES

6 Rome or Winesap apples
1 cup brown sugar
2 tsps. cinnamon

⅓ cup raisins
¼ cup cinnamon candy
(red hots)
12 T. maple syrup

Core apples most of the way through, but leave the bottom intact. Trim a small slice off the stem end of the apples. Stuff them with a mixture of the brown sugar, cinnamon, raisins and candy. Place apples in 2-inch deep baking dish and pour about 2 T. of maple syrup over each. Bake uncovered in a preheated 375 degree oven, 35 to 40 minutes or until they are brown and soft. Serve with half and half.

Betty Bauer   Mission Viejo, California

CREAM WAFFLES

2 eggs
1¾ cups milk
½ cup butter, melted
2 cups sifted flour

4 tsps. baking powder
½ tsp. salt
1 T.

Beat eggs; add remaining ingredients and continue beating until smooth. Bake in heated waffle iron. Do not stir batter between bakings. Chopped nuts may also be added to the batter.

Bill Kelly   Holland, Michigan

STRAWBERRY PRESERVES

1 quart strawberries
2 tsps. vinegar

4 cups sugar

Wash and stem strawberries. Add vinegar and cook 3 minutes. Add sugar and bring to a full rolling boil. Cook 10 minutes. Skim. Place in shallow pan or dish overnight. When ready to jar, place jars, lids and rings in boiling water. Fill drained, hot jars with preserves and seal immediately with hot lids. Yields 2 pints.

Carolyn Slocum   Tulsa, Oklahoma

HOT BUTTERED RUM MIX

1 lb. butter, melted
1 lb. white granulated sugar
1 lb. dark brown sugar

½ pint vanilla ice cream
   softened
1 tsp. vanilla

Melt butter. Add white sugar, brown sugar and 1 tsp. vanilla. Cool. Combine with ½ pt. ice cream. Store in plastic container and freeze. Keeps all winter. To prepare hot buttered rum, place generous tsp. of mix in mug. Add 1 jigger rum, and fill with boiling water.

Louise Brady   Cape Giardeau, Missouri

HERB BUTTER

1 T. herbs

¼ lb. softened butter or
   margarine

1 T. of the minced herb is mixed into ¼ lb. softened butter or margarine. Let stand at room temperature for at least one hour or more. After flavor has been absorbed into butter it should be chilled. This will keep if covered tightly in refrigerator.

Kathy Kaczinski   Dewitt, Iowa

QUICK QUICHE—TO MICROWAVE

1 can (13 oz.) evaporated milk
½ tsp. seasoned salt
6 eggs, beaten
¼ cup chopped green pepper

2 tsps. instant minced onion
8 oz. shredded Cheddar cheese
   (about 2 cups)
2 T. diced pimiento

1 baked 9-inch piecrust, cooled

In microwave-safe bowl, combine milk, onion and salt. Microwave on high power 3 minutes, stirring after 1½ minutes. Stir in cheese. Microwave on high power 1 minute, stirring after 30 seconds. Stir again and let set about 1 minute until cheese melts. Stir 1 T. of cheese mixture into beaten eggs. Mix well. Slowly add beaten eggs. Mix well. Slowly add beaten egg mixture into remaining cheese mixture. Mix in green pepper and pimiento. Pour into pie shell. Microwave on high power 5 minutes, turning dish ½ turn after 2¼ minutes. Lower power to 50% or 30% and microwave 8 to 12 minutes longer, turning dish ¼ turn 2 or 3 times to assure even cooking. Center will appear slightly shaky. Let dish set uncovered 10 minutes to firm up quiche. To serve; cut into wedges. Note: If using packaged frozen piecrust, deep-dish 9-inch size needed. Serves 6-8.

Beverly Bradley   Moline, Illinois